JOURNEY TO ARCHITECTURE

College Admissions & Profiles

Rachel A. Winston, Ph.D.

ISBN 978-1946432674 (hardback); 978-1946432667 (paperback); 978-1946432681 (e-book)

LCCN: 2022906537

Lizard Publishing, 7700 Irvine Center Drive, Suite 800, Irvine, CA 92618 *www.lizard-publishing.com*

Lizard Publishing creates, designs, produces, and distributes books and resources to provide academic, admissions, and career information. Our mental process is fueled by three tenets:

- Ignite the hunger to learn and the passion to make a difference
- Illuminate the expanse of knowledge by sharing cutting edge thinking
- Innovate to create a world that makes the transition from dreams to reality

We work with academic leaders who transform the educational landscape to publish relevant content and advise students of their educational and professional options, with the aim of developing 21st-century learners and leaders. We also work with students to publish their books and present widely diverse ideas to the college/graduate school-bound community. With headquarters in Irvine, California, Lizard Publishing works virtually with authors to edit, publish, and distribute both hard copy and paperback books.

This book was published in the U.S.A. Lizard Publishing is a premium quality provider of educational reference, career guidance, and motivational publications/merchandise for global learners, educators, and stakeholders in education.

Book design by Michelle Tahan *www.michelletahan.com*

Book formatting by Obinna Chinemerem Ozuo

Book website: *www.collegelizard.com*

LIZARD PUBLISHING

This book is dedicated to Yanjun ("Emily") Liu, who epitomizes dedication, multi-dimensional talent, and professionalism.

ACKNOWLEDGMENTS

There is never enough room to acknowledge every person. Numerous people contributed to my perspective about architecture. Students, faculty, counselors, and researchers assisted in enhancing my knowledge base or taught me indelible lessons. Over a lifetime of experiences working with students, I am wiser and more worldly.

I gratefully acknowledge Michelle Tahan, Jasmine Jhunjhnuwala, E. Liz Kim, and Jacqueline Xu, as well as my family, friends, colleagues, and professors. With profound gratitude, I also acknowledge those I have known in the architecture world.

As a faculty member in the UCLA College Counseling Certificate Program, I met many dedicated counselors who spend their life serving and supporting students. Meaningful contributions to the book have been made indirectly by admissions representatives, college counselors, and faculty members who took a special interest in this book's success.

I would also like to thank the thousands of students I have taught, counseled, or supported in my nearly four decades of service.

> *"If I see so far, it is because I stand on the shoulders of giants."*
> *— Isaac Newton*

Isaac Newton once said, "If I see so far, it is because I stand on the shoulders of giants." A few of those giants whose broad shoulders lifted me higher and helped teach invaluable lessons include: Siyu Chen, Yan Zerui, Alex Liu, Ryan La, Serafina Raskin, Nina Ardalan, Samantha Mann, Sharon Cruz-McKinney, Jacquelyn Lingelbach, Ryan Hubner, Christina Ryan, Jeff To, Jennifer Dal Poggetto, Bonyen Thomas, Leyla Samimi, Cara Ludutsky, Joanna Ricardi, and Ron Herrick.

Finally, there would be no book on architecture schools and no career college admissions counseling without the support of Robert Helmer, whose tireless efforts support me every single day.

ABOUT THE AUTHOR

D r. Rachel A. Winston is a tireless student advocate. She has served the educational community as a university professor, college advisor, statistician, researcher, author, cryptanalyst, motivational speaker, publishing executive, and lifelong student. As one of the leading experts in college counseling and an award-winning faculty member, Dr. Winston has spent her lifetime learning, teaching, mentoring, and coaching students. Her counseling practice centers around college admissions, college essays, portfolios, and intellectual conversations about life and career pursuits.

She started college at thirteen and graduated from college programs in such widely ranging disciplines as chemistry, mathematics, computers, liberal arts, international relations, negotiation, conflict resolution, peacebuilding, business administration, higher education leadership, interpreting, college counseling, and publishing. Throughout her education, she attended and graduated from Harvard, University of Chicago, University of Texas, GWU, UCLA, Syracuse, CSUF, CSUDH, Pepperdine, Claremont Graduate University, and Gallaudet University.

Her position working in Washington, D.C. on Capitol Hill and with the White House in the 1980s took her to approximately a hundred universities training campaign managers at colleges from Colorado to California, thoroughly dotting the western states. Later, she led college tours with students and their families on road trips throughout the United States. She has taught or counseled thousands of students over her career and speaks at conferences and academic programs throughout the world.

As a professor and avid writer for numerous publications, she won the 2012 McFarland Literary Achievement Award, Bletchley Park Cryptanalyst Award, and numerous other awards, including Faculty Member of the Year, Leadership Tomorrow Leader of the Year, and college service and leadership awards. While studying Human Capital at Claremont Graduate University, she was a scholarship recipient at the Drucker School of Management. She was also elected to the statewide Board of Governors for the Faculty Association for California Community Colleges, where she served on their executive committee.

She also served as a faculty member for the UCLA College Counselor Certificate Program, the Director of Mathematics at Brandman University, and Embry Riddle Aeronautical University, Chapman University, Cal State Fullerton, and a handful of California Community Colleges, including Cerro Coso College where she represented the entire faculty as the Academic Senate President and retired in 2016. Over her career, she taught mathematics online, on television, live interactive satellite, telecourses, and in large and small lecture halls.

AUTHOR'S NOTE

You are reading this book because you are considering admission to colleges where you open the doors to the world of architecture. Whatever route you took to get to this point, you are in the right place. Right now, you need to gather information to make informed decisions.

While many people offer advice, suggestions differ. Friends will tell you the 'right' way or the way their neighbor was accepted. Graciously accept this anecdotal information, pursuing architecture with your heart and mind as you commit to learning more.

Dig deeper to consider both expert and current information from counselors who have worked with hundreds of students. Changes in programs, curricula, requirements, and links happen each year.

Doublecheck each program's specifics yourself. Each school's profile information is current as of March 2022. However, since researching this book, changes may have taken place. There are other college guidebooks written by talented and experienced counselors, though none like this book on architecture. Nevertheless, I admire and cheer on their efforts.

> *"We are what we think. All that we are arises with our thoughts. With our thoughts, we make the world."*
> — *Buddha*

This book, providing lists of colleges, admissions information, and profiles, is different in that it also offers unique tidbits. I hope you find the information valuable. Your job is to begin early by assembling lists of possible schools to consider. Create a road map and set yourself on a clear path.

If you see an error in this book or even a suggestion for a future edition, please write to Dr. Rachel A. Winston at collegeguide@yahoo.com. We will fix the entry with the next printed version. All of that said, this book was written with you in mind.

This book contains a wealth of information on the Internet with free downloads, FAQs, testimonials, and offers to help you with your applications. Some of these advisors are knowledgeable and can help you. Unfortunately, students and parents hunt around the web, searching for a tremendous number of hours to seek the information they need. This book aims to resolve this problem with college admissions data and profiles to make your search easier.

For now, though, we will assume you want to attend college to study architecture and are exploring this book to find a program that will get you on your way toward your goal. You are undoubtedly a talented candidate who is willing to work very hard. Selflessly collaborating is virtually a prerequisite for architecture programs.

As you investigate colleges, you might find that some programs are listed in different college departments. Either way, this book will help you reach your goal. Applying to and writing essays for each application will require research to determine which program is right for you and the specific reasons you are a good fit.

While you might believe that architecture schools are relatively similar, each program's nuances make them very different. These small differences may seem confusing. My goal with this book is to demystify the information and process.

CONTENTS

RETHINKING ARCHITECTURE, CONSTRUCTION, AND URBAN DESIGN: BUILDING A FOUNDATION FOR THE FUTURE

"When I'm working on a problem, I never think about beauty. But when I've finished, if the solution is not beautiful... I know it's wrong."

– Buckminster Fuller

"Architecture is about trying to make the world a little more like our dreams."

– Bjarke Ingels

Architecture's role in society is immensely important and underappreciated. Outside and inside of lived spaces is an organization of life constructed by city planners and architects. Committed to the creation of buildings, communities, and shared environments, architects invent the future. From the city's master plan to the plants lining regional walkways, architects savor a job well-done while individuals go about their daily business.

With innovations in technology, energy, and communication, soon people will not use a land telephone line in much the same way people no longer type on a typewriter. Our walls will become massive computer monitors, bathroom mirrors will have embedded televisions, and building materials will be stronger, thinner, and more durable than ever.

This moment is exciting. Technological innovation is disrupting every facet of life. Thus, we live in a time when rapid change will require that we think differently. The future of humanity and all other living things depends on planners and architects.

You are living at a critical juncture where 5G, 6G, and 7G will mesh with digital currencies and metaverse spaces. We will barely recognize our current existence by 2050. Much of that transformation will happen as a function of architects who will engineer tomorrow's landscapes and skyline. Architectural innovation is the solution to affordable housing, overcrowded cities, and land depletion.

Architects, on the cutting edge of material science, automated drone construction, and augmented reality have the foresight and power to transform society into a place we want to live. With efficient transportation corridors, lifestyle conveniences, and entertainment arenas, this live-learn-work-evolve environment awaits. In essence, city planners and architects will re-imagine life.

USING ENGINEERING METHODS TO AWE AND INSPIRE

A city's twinkling lights, dimmed after a long bustling day of work, retain their magic in a process that takes place around the dials of timepiece. Like clockwork, urban centers electrify. The energy of people rushing to and fro may be hushed for now but will awaken soon enough. This process begins and ends in our living spaces where we, too, dim the lights in the evening and wipe our eyes in the morning, refreshed from our necessary moments of rest.

In studio spaces, creativity is unleashed. Architects, inspired to invent the future, blend vision and wonder with the nuts and bolts of technical drawing and fabrication. Students studying architecture are invited to set free the barriers of their minds-eye and imagine what has yet to be considered.

Space, limiting to some, is merely a given entity in which to create. No matter how little cement, how many intersecting byways, or how complex the natural environment, architects overcome the challenges and invent the future. Physical space and environmental limitations are conquered, pushing back on developers whose profit-centered mentality often urges speed and budget over design and engineering.

CLIMATE CHANGE, POLITICAL STRIFE, AND ENGINEERING INNOVATION

The trifecta of uncertainty can be summed up in the tsunami of sociocultural and transformational change.

1. Climate Change
2. Political Strife
3. Engineering Innovation

Overwhelming evidence portends dynamic change on the horizon. Sea levels are rising. Social tensions rage in cities and countries. A wave of engineering advances is rapidly percolating in university and industrial research labs. You sit at this most exciting, yet harrowing juncture where you can make a difference. Your role is to envision and create tomorrow today.

CHALLENGES AHEAD

According to the Environmental Protection Agency (EPA), while absolute sea levels are rising 0.12 – 0.14 inches per year, relative sea levels are not uniform. New York City has 578 miles of shoreline with most of its inhabitants within a mile of its waterfront. Planning agencies in New York are mitigating for "managed retreat". While sandbags, berms, dams, and barriers will work in the short term, city planners and architects are working with agencies to mollify this problem. The National Oceanic and Atmospheric Administration (NOAA) estimates the prognosis for Miami is worse. So, how can architects help to create entirely new cities in the wake of unprecedented flooding?

In envisioning a new tomorrow and rebuilding the cities of today, we must prepare for climate change, population growth, challenges in delivery pipelines, and sustainable practices to support people's lives and livelihoods. Furthermore, today's unsustainable waste practices must shift to repurpose and reuse options which might pose an opportunity for planners and builders. Also, for many people, security is paramount in their living and working spaces. As a result, college academic programs offer a myriad of ways to view today's safety and protection challenges, while designing next-gen possibilities to invent a new tomorrow.

A FEW FACTS TO CONSIDER

- Poverty, inflation, war, and disease increased global food insecurity.
- Africa's population is expected to double by 2050.
- Supply chains, transportation mechanisms, and limiting factors of non-renewable resources will threaten populations.
- Oceans are dying due to overfishing, pollution, and environmental change.
- Many islands and some U.S. cities are likely to be partially underwater by 2050. According to NOAA, Miami's sea level is 8 inches higher now than in 1950.
- Global angst, propaganda mechanisms, and philosophical divisions threaten to widen the fissure between people.

HOPE AND PRAGMATISM

An architect's work exists at the intersection of hope and pragmatism. By rethinking brick-and-mortar buildings and considering automated, flexible, multipurpose space design, the possibilities are limitless. You will build the foundation for civilization's future. Begin this journey by stepping into the possibilities of today and developing the augmented realities of tomorrow.

There are many directions you can take with architecture. The programs at each of the colleges profiled in this book offered varied paths to licensure, design, planning, development, and management. The future is yours. Choose the path that makes sense for your life goals. The information contained within will lead you on your way.

If you invest in beauty, it will remain with you all the days of your life.

- Frank Lloyd Wright

CHAPTER 2

EXPECTATIONS AND TRAINING: DESIGN-CENTERED, ENVIRONMENTALLY-CONSCIOUS THINKING

"You never stop learning."

– **Norman Foster**

Architects design and build structures in a way that is structurally sound and aesthetically pleasing, while considering other factors like being safe, functional, sustainable, efficient, and economically viable. While the task may seem basic, the field requires the knowledge of civil engineering, material science, environmental planning, computer-aided design, aesthetics, and urban development, along with project design, programming, management, construction, analysis, and evaluation. The combination of these complex topics adds to the challenge and intrigue of this career path.

ARCHI – "CHIEF" AND TECT – "CREATOR"

The Greek origins of the word architecture emphasize the importance of the profession throughout history and the expression of a society's culture. From the time 1st-century Roman architect, Vitruvius, wrote the 10-book standard treatise, *De architectura*, used by architects for centuries to today, architecture has become deeply steeped in science as well as art.

Cultural icons, preserving the essence of civilization's history, tower over cities with their ornamental domes, grand towers, vaulted ceilings, and marble columns. Awe-inspiring structures like the Great Wall of China, the Parthenon on the Acropolis, the Roman Coliseum, the Egyptian Pyramids, and the Vatican draw hundreds of thousands of visitors each year.

The durability of ancient buildings, sustaining the tests of time, underscores what 19th-century American architect, Louis Sullivan, explained as "form follows function". Sullivan's influence in the Chicago School was profound as he is often called the "father of skyscrapers".

Modern architecture is somewhat different than its ancient predecessors, presenting a more minimalist, streamlined version. Much of America's architecture, built in the 20th-century, integrates utilitarian design elements in 90-degree angles with concrete and steel. Meanwhile, 21st-century contemporary architecture has no single paradigm, though many architects moved away from the horizontal and vertical lines of the past century to more curved and non-linear models.

Increasingly, contemporary architecture incorporates Green thinking with more sustainable designs and materials with natural light and airflow. Some of today's extraordinary Platinum LEED-rated buildings include King St. Station in Seattle, the Vancouver Convention Center, Taipei 101 in Taiwan, and the Lawrence Convention Center in Pittsburgh. In the future, most buildings are likely to incorporate natural air, light, and energy.

The U.S. Green Building Council developed a Leadership in Energy and Environmental Design (LEED) rating system, used widely throughout the world. With the goal to reduce carbon emissions and address issues related to climate change and sustainability, LEED aids architects and procurement managers alike in assessing buildings designs.

LEED RATINGS
Certified (40-49 points); Silver (50-59 points); Gold (60-79 points); and Platinum (80+ points)

As students infuse environmental consciousness into society and more research centers develop stronger and more durable materials, new architects will inject noticeable changes in design, efficiency, and sustainability. Bachelor's-level university architecture training in B.Arch. programs require a minimum of 150-semester hours. The master's level, M.Arch., requires approximately 90 – 130 semester credits. University course and experience requirements are set by the National Architectural Accrediting Board (NAAB).

With the need to master concepts across a broad set of subjects, expanded due to engineering innovation and regulations, architects develop numerous proficiencies. Starting with theoretical underpinnings, students go on to consider external structure and material possibilities as well as internal mechanics, power, plumbing, and spatial dynamics. Design studios offer the space to imagine and invent unique architecture.

THE ART & SCIENCE OF ARCHITECTURE

In B.Arch. and M.Arch. programs, students should expect to spend long hours in studios independently and on collaborative projects. The synergy and energy can be electrifying as projects take shape and masterful designs propel ideas to a whole new level. However, there is much to learn about social conditions, water systems, sewage considerations, and engineering marvels.

Despite the structure of science, creativity is fundamental to the work. Ultimately, the jigsaw puzzle of building elements, magnificently blending art and science, will seamlessly fit together, connecting its moving parts. Yet, with a limited timeframe and compact space, clarity and design have its bounds. You will learn how to manage time and quickly evaluate the status of your projects.

Collaborating can be both challenging and exhilarating at the same time. Each member must listen attentively and conceptualize options in 2-D and 3-D space while proposing ideas and creating a clear line of communication. By discussing opportunities for improvement, pitfalls in design elements, and financial and spatial limitations, the team can efficiently and effectively cooperate to craft the best representation of the design.

NEVER-ENDING FASCINATION

You will learn about history, geography, politics, and society alongside building eco-friendly environments. Every region holds its unique opportunities and challenges. Furthermore, zoning restrictions can be a big factor in the success of a project. Securing materials, mitigating landscape factors, and working to obtain permits can be impediments or they can open new doors to partnerships. Experience makes a difference as young, brilliant, and eager neophytes seek to be recognized for their talents in a field where longevity, respect, and wisdom are not acquired quickly.

The journey you are taking will have its ups and downs, but you will have stories to tell for the rest of your life. Your education may have unpredictable elements and pitfalls may lay in your path. Since you have endured a pandemic and the repercussions of a war, you are imbued with a few doses of resilience. Even so, you will be tested in architecture school as there is much to learn and a short amount of time.

You are embarking on a thrilling, demanding, and disciplined pursuit. You will work with extremely skilled and brilliant students who started studying science and drawing complex images when they entered elementary school. Some have worked in architecture offices and will blow you away with their abilities. However, rarely are there architecture students equally skilled in all areas. Some of your work will be a team effort where everyone will contribute what they know. You will too.

Some classmates will be amazingly talented. Do not let their abilities bring you down or make you feel as if you are not good enough. You will add your element and learn more during college. Besides, your enthusiasm for architecture will show through in your work and effort. Recognizing your potential, commitment, and attitude, people will be awed at your creations as you also step back to appreciate your work.

Enjoy the experience.

Don't judge each day by the harvest you reap but by the seeds that you plant

- Robert Louis Stevenson

CHAPTER 3

ACADEMIC PREPARATION: ART AND SCIENCE FOUNDATION FOR FUTURE COURSEWORK

"Freedom is from within."

– Frank Lloyd Wright

"If you fail to plan, you are planning to fail."

- Benjamin Franklin

The moment is now. You are on a course toward STEAM (STEM + Art) mastery. To gain admission you must be smart in science and talented in design. Even if the admission's requirements do not require a portfolio, and many do, to be successful, there are numerous preparatory skills you must develop as if you were presenting your work to a committee. Plan for your future now. Talent is only the beginning.

In high school, or college if you plan to transfer into a program, you must build solid science skills in science and math. Physics, chemistry, and calculus are almost always a prerequisite. More is better. However, you must also be talented in art.

Some mix of drawing, painting, ceramics, sculpture, 3-D design, and digital art are key components of a portfolio, though not all of these skills are necessary. Some applicants have never taken classes in 3-D design or architectural drawing are not penalized for this. Nevertheless, foundational skills in graphics, design, and art theory are important.

Computer programming classes are a definite plus. Further, architectural design necessitates a strong foundation in computer graphics and technical drawing. You are walking into a future where virtual reality and augmented reality will require greater technology skills than applicants even ten years ago when most architects created 2-D renderings that were often difficult to visualize. Yet, as you enter college, technology's rapid advancements will transform from primarily 2-D drawings to primarily 3-D virtual reality graphics.

VISUALIZE, COMMUNICATE, EXECUTE

The power and promise of 5G, 6G, and 7G will advance science and art in revolutionary rather than evolutionary ways. Computing power, many times faster than today, will allow for quick permutations of design options and animations never before possible. Teams will collaborate on holograms of buildings designed together in a shared space with members who need not be physically present.

Clearly visualized 3-D animations of designs using virtual reality will allow customers and patrons to take a walk-through of a building not yet created. Augmented reality will add to this experience by providing the viewer a user experience, possibly, one day, in the metaverse. These environments can be constructed and fully automated with computer design and programming tools. Group members will be able to adapt designs in quick iterations, allowing for a near-real visualization of the physical model as each person analyzes form and function of each space.

Translation and implementation of the construction design can be witnessed and managed, since every built part will be computerized and visualized without the necessity of manual paper and audio call updates. Automated processes will be more efficient without the requirements of frequent construction site visits.

A 3-D PRINTER IN EVERY SCHOOL

While 3-D printing machines were initially developed in the 1980s for rapid prototyping, a decade ago, the broader public got a glimpse of a desktop model by MakerBot, a company, that envisioned a 3-D printer in every home. Tens of thousands of guests at the 2012 Consumer Electronics Show (CES) witnessed the creation of plastic parts created in front of them. I highly recommend going to CES if you get the chance. The show is three days of tantalizing inspiration for the maker in you. Nevertheless, what started as an expensive novelty machine changed its market focus when Stratasys purchased MakerBot and realigned its sales and distribution strategy toward the technology and education markets.

Most colleges of architecture have access to 3-D printers in their fabrication spaces. At one point or another, while studying architecture, 3-D printing will come into play. Projects are likely to include fabricating buildings, bridges, and shopping areas. You may also be asked to design interior environments with furniture using filament in a wide variety of colors with matte, silk, shiny, or transparent and finishes resembling wood, cardboard, and an assortment of metals. Some filaments even glow in the dark while others change color based upon temperature. Imagine the extraordinary possibilities.

The point about 3-D printing, holograms, virtual reality, and augmented reality spaces is that any training you can do now in design, CAD, maker spaces, architectural drawings, computer science, and digital arts will be extremely helpful. Find a location where you can experiment with these new technologies or volunteer in any way at an architectural firm. Even if all you do is get coffee for people during your volunteer service, you will gain invaluable lessons as you watch how the firm ticks.

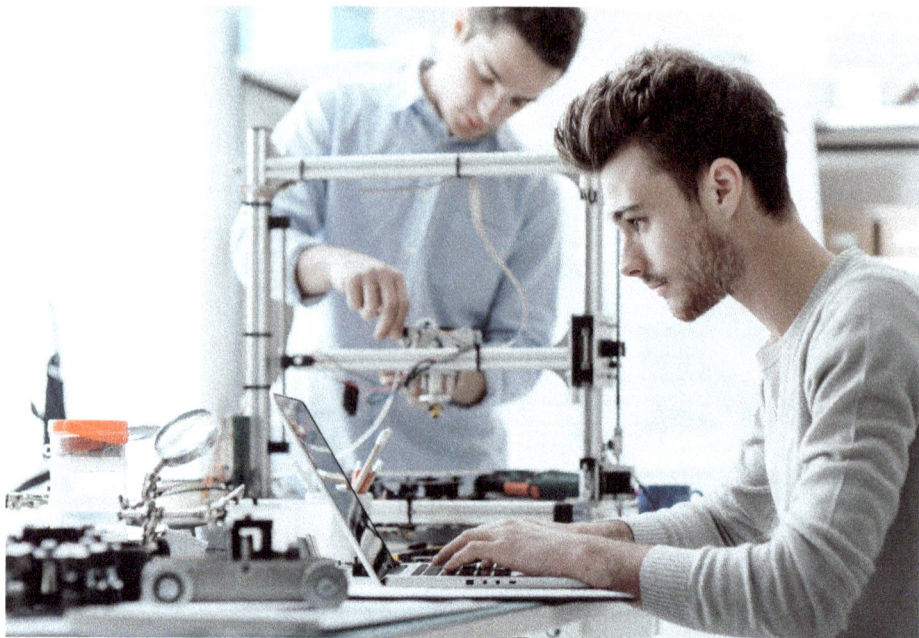

Even if the classes you want to take are not offered at your school, there are summer camps, short-term programs, online training, maker clubs, and college classes that would help you immensely along your way. Additional science classes would not hurt you at all either. Knowledge of chemistry and physics is imperative. The more you know, the more you will be able to access the information necessary to be a design guru.

Additionally, there is no way to understate the value of even a basic understanding of robotics. Building, programming, and working with robots in high school will help you while you are in college. Join or create a robotics team. See if there is a regional robotics club or league. If neither of these is available, find an avid robotics student and have them help you start from scratch.

Finally, William James Durant and his wife, Ariel, wrote a nearly 11,000-page tome called "The Story of Civilization" in which they broke down history into events that captured the ideas and philosophy of the time. One of his sayings was, "Science is organized knowledge. Wisdom is organized life." You will efficiently and effectively collect massive amounts of knowledge and invent your future with wisdom and passion.

Science unveils the mystery of the universe, and everything contained within can be explained by its principles. Thus, as you embark on your journey, learn as much as you can about science and mathematics, remembering that making a game plan now and challenging yourself to learn new and often difficult subjects is the first step along that journey.

"Mathematics is the language in which God has written the universe."

Galileo

"*Philosophy is written in that great book which ever lies before our eyes — I mean the universe — but we cannot understand it if we do not first learn the language and grasp the symbols, in which it is written. This book is written in the mathematical language, and the symbols are triangles, circles and other geometrical figures, without whose help it is impossible to comprehend a single word of it; without which one wanders in vain through a dark labyrinth." - Galileo*

– *The Assayer* (1623), translated by Thomas Salusbury (1661)

CHAPTER 4

ARCHITECTURE AND DESIGN EXPERIENCES: INTERNSHIPS AND PROGRAMS FOR HIGH SCHOOL AND COLLEGE STUDENTS

"Ignorance is bliss...with this innocence you can create and question a lot of things."

– Kunle Adeyemi

S tart early to gain architecture and design experiences. Internships and summer programs are as important along your educational pathway as coursework. The lessons you learn from working collaboratively and collegially with other design-focused mentors may be different but equally important. Historian and scholar, W.E.B. DuBois (1868-1963), a founding member of the NAACP and the first Black American to earn a Ph.D. at Harvard said, "Education must not simply teach work - it must teach life." Your college, experiential, and career education go hand-in-hand, driven by purpose and foresight since life truly is a journey, not a destination.

SUMMER ARCHITECTURE CAMPS FOR HIGH SCHOOL STUDENTS

ALABAMA

Auburn University – Architecture Camp - School of Architecture, Planning and Landscape Architecture Studios

> 1-week; 3 Sessions – Full Scholarships Available (apply by April 1)
>
> This highly-intensive, hands-on program begins with basic concepts.
>
> Students produce architectural designs, working directly with professors.
>
> Camp counselors support students with 24/7 questions, safety, and supervision.

Tuskegee University Taylor School of Architecture & Construction Science (TSACS)

> Virtual Preview of Architecture and Construction at Tuskegee (V-PACT) 3-hour Virtual Program
>
> Preview Architecture & Construction Science 2-week Program

ARIZONA
Arcosanti – Re-Imagined Urbanism

Building resilient, equitable, integrated, and sustainable communities.

6-week core curriculum and discussion-based classes/training on erosion control, composting, agriculture, and more.

Combining architecture and ecology (arcology), you can learn in the World's First Prototype Arcology.

Core values: (1) Frugality and Resourcefulness, (2) Ecological Accountability, (3) Experiential Learning, and (4) Leaving a Limited Footprint. Arcosanti's eco-conscious model seeks solutions countering mass consumerism, urban sprawl, unchecked consumption, and social isolation.

ARKANSAS
University of Arkansas

Design Camp – In-Person Grades 9-12 – 1-week in Fayetteville

Design projects, studio groups, tours, meetings with local designers, and discussions on architecture and design.

Virtual Design Camp (School-guided): students Grades 8-12

No fee; completely remote; design camp lessons embedded; students are paired with a faculty member in a studio group.

Advanced Design Camp: students entering Grades 11-12, 2-weeks in Fayetteville (multiple dates)

Camp led by Fay Jones School faculty and students.

CALIFORNIA
Architectural Foundation of San Francisco

Build SF Summer Design Institute 3-week fun, fast-paced program for HS students.

Students receive instruction on digital design software platforms; present original work.

Receive feedback and participate in collaborative activities; creating a digital portfolio for college and internships.

Individual mentoring with an architect or engineer.

Need-based financial aid is available.

Girls Garage (gender-expansive queer, trans, non-binary, non-conforming youth) - Berkeley

Advanced Design/Build – Grade 9-12 – Free

Young Women's Design and Building Institute – Grades 9-12 – Free

Builder Bootcamp – July – Grades 5-8; $425 (scholarships available)

La Jolla Historical Society

Young Architects Summer Program – Grades 7–12; two 5-day sessions

Middle School student program and High School student program

Learn space and layout planning, develop architectural drawing, modeling, and computer skills.

Learn about La Jolla's residential communities; students design structures with Sketch-Up with specific criteria.

Students present their PPT presentations to the class and parents (taught by practicing architects).

SCI-Arc Immersive 4-week Summer Program (Design Immersion Days) – Los Angeles

Southern California Institute of Architecture

Introduction to the academic and professional world of architecture – Grades 9-12

UCLA Summer Jumpstart Summer Institute – Introduction to Architecture – Los Angeles

4-week program in the Department of Architecture and Urban Design (must have HS diploma).

Portfolio development for architecture, design, and related fields – 6 UC quarter units.

Intensive design, CAD, 3-D modeling

USC Architecture Pre-College Programs – Los Angeles

A-Lab Architecture Development Program – High School Architecture Program

Exploration of Architecture – 4-week program, 3 college credits

DISTRICT OF COLUMBIA
Catholic University School of Architecture and Planning

Summer High School Program - 2-week Residential (Two Session Options)

FLORIDA
Florida Atlantic University – Boca Raton, FL and Ft. Lauderdale, FL

School of Architecture – July (Three Session Options)

July 3-week program for rising sophomores, juniors, seniors, and first 2 years of college.

Certificate of Completion Awarded – Enrollment on a first-come, first-served basis.

Portfolio development, fabrication, architectural education, portfolio display, critique

University of Florida Design Exploration Program (DEP)

3-week Residential Immersion into the architectural studio environment.

Construction of studio design projects, teamwork, seminars, field trips, architectural theory.

University of Miami Summer Scholars, Explorations in Architecture & Design– Coral Gables, FL

3-week Residential program; 6 college credits; Design, Graphics, and Theory.

Architecture, Landscape Architecture, Historic Preservation; Urban Planning.

Studio experience with drawing, model making, drafting, CAD, visual analysis.

GEORGIA

Georgia Institute of Technology Pre-College Design Program – Atlanta, GA

2-week Residential program – College of Design – Grades 11 & 12 (Two Session Options)

Architecture, building construction, industrial design, and music technology

Savannah College of Art & Design – Savannah, GA

SCAD Rising Star – rising HS senior – SCAD coursework

Week-long Summer Seminars – Grades 10-12

2-week Residential program – College of Design – Grades 11 & 12 (Two Session Options)

ILLINOIS

Frank Lloyd Wright Trust Summer Design Camps

1-day (June) Grades 3-5 Design, build, and innovate in the drafting room of Frank Lloyd Wright's Oak Park Studio.

1-day (July) Grades 6-8 Design, build, and innovate in the drafting room of Frank Lloyd Wright's Oak Park Studio.

Illinois Institute of Technology Summer Introduction to Architecture

2-week Experiment in Architecture for HS students – Comprehensive overview

1-week Exploration in Architecture for middle school students – studio-based, firm visits, field trips, and projects.

Judson University Architecture and Interior Design – Design Discovery Summer Workshop (July – HS students)

Live on campus; experience studio classes; visit firms in Chicago; discover more about architecture & interior design.

School of the Art Institute of Chicago – Early College Program for HS Students

1-, 2-, 4-week Residential programs in painting, drawing, animation, comics/graphic novels, fashion, design.

Portfolio development programs; earn college credit.

Full tuition scholarships are available.

Southern Illinois University Carbondale – Kid Architecture

1-week (June) Elementary Grades

1-week (July) Middle School Architecture Camp

1-week (July) High School Architecture Camp

University of Illinois at Chicago Architecture at Chicago College of Architecture, Design, and the Arts HiArch Summer High School Program

> 1-, 2-week (July) - HS students are introduced to the culture of architecture, design, thinking, and making.

INDIANA
University of Notre Dame School of Architecture – Career Discovery: Architecture

> 12-day (June/July) HS Students - Experience life as an ND architecture student.
>
> Participating in design studios, architecture seminars, and field trips.

IOWA
Iowa State University – College of Design - HS Design Camps

> 1-week HS Students – Architecture, studio/fine arts, regional planning, graphic design, interior design, industrial design, and landscape architecture.

MARYLAND
Maryland Institute College of Art (MICA) – Baltimore, MD

> 2-, 3-, 5-week HS Students – Live instruction, studio time, workshops, artist talks, collaboration, feedback, critique, and evaluation.

MASSACHUSETTS
Boston Architectural College Early College Program - Boston, MA

> 4-week (July) Residential Program – HS Students – Live lectures, site visits, hands-on design, and team building.
>
> BAC's VDI CloudLab; sketchbook; develop physical design portfolio.

Harvard University GSD Design Discovery– Cambridge, MA (Ages 18-mid-career professionals)

> 3-week Residential Program – Architecture, Landscape, Urban Planning & Design.
>
> Physical modeling, fabrication, and assembly.

Massachusetts Institute of Technology – Urbaneframe – Cambridge, MA

> HS Students - Summer Design-Build Project
>
> CAD, drafting, sketching, mapping and context study, historical research, and carpentry & construction.

University of Massachusetts Amherst Pre-College – Amherst, MA

1-, 2-, 3-week Residential Intensives Grades 10-12

3-D Design, 3-D Animation, Building & Construction Technology; Combatting the Climate Crisis

Summer Engineering Institute, Summer Design Academy, Programming for Aspiring Scientists

Wellesley College – Wellesley, MA

2-week Residential Program - EXPLO Pre-College + Career for Grades 10-12

Three session options; Topics include – AI, Entrepreneurship, Engineering, Medicine, Law, CSI

MICHIGAN

Andrews University School of Architecture & Interior Design - Renaissance Kids – Berrien Springs, MI

Virtual Studio Projects, lecture, community build projects

Lawrence Technological University Marburger STEM Center - Southfield, MI

1-week Residential Camps – Data Analysis, Design Studio/Architecture, Digital Media, Landscape Architecture

Industrial Engineering, 3-D Modeling & Printing; Sketching & Visual Communication

University of Michigan – Taubman College of Architecture – ArcStart

4-week (June/July)– HS Students

MISSOURI

Washington University in St. Louis Architecture Discovery Program & Portfolio Development Program

Sam Fox School of Design & Visual Arts – Design Studio program; design thinking; architecture project

2-week (July) Rigorous Residential Architecture Program – Grades 11 & 12

University of Missouri, Kansas City – Department of Architecture, Urban Planning & Design MA

Design Discovery Program – Architecture, Interior Design, Landscape Architecture

3-day (July) Non-Residential Program – HS Students/Current College Students

NEBRASKA
University of Nebraska College of Architecture – Lincoln, NE

6-day (June) Residential Program – Grades 11 & 12 – Studio training, architectural design, scholarships

NEW JERSEY
New Jersey Institute of Technology – Hillier College of Architecture & Design

1-week (July) Residential Program – HS Students – Architecture, Interior Design, Industrial Design, Digital Design

Summer Architecture + Design Programs (2 Start Dates)

NEW YORK
AIA New York – Center for Architecture

1-week (July) Residential Program – HS Students – Architecture

Programs for Grades 3-12 include Architectural Design Studio, Drawing Architecture, Rooftop Dwelling, Dream House, and Treehouses.

Skyscrapers, Green Island Home, Subway Architecture, Waterfront City, Parks & Playground Design, and Neighborhood Design.

City University of New York – Spitzer School of Architecture

Career Lab exposes students to college-level architectural study; workshops are provided in architectural portfolios.

Columbia University - New York, NY – Graduate School of Architecture, Planning, and Preservation

5-week July-August Residential Program (remote also)– College Students – Portfolio Preparation for Grad School

Cooper Union - New York, NY – Chanin School of Architecture (Programs for HS & College Students)

4-, 5-week July-August Online & Residential Programs

Introduction to Architecture; Digital Fabrication Summer Program: Design-Build Education

28

Cornell University – Ithaca, NY – Precollege Studies

3-, 6-, 9-week June-August Residential Program

ARCH 1110 Introduction to Architecture: Design Studio and ARCH 1300 Lectures

ARCH 1419 Introduction to Topics in Architecture, Culture, and Society and ARCH 1518 Architectural Representation

ARCH 1618 Introduction to Topics in Architectural Science & Technology

Rensselaer Polytechnic University – Troy, NY

Architecture Career Discovery Program

Syracuse University – Syracuse, NY – On-Campus and Online Programs for HS Students

2-, 6-week programs in Architecture, Design Studies and Environmental & Interior Design.

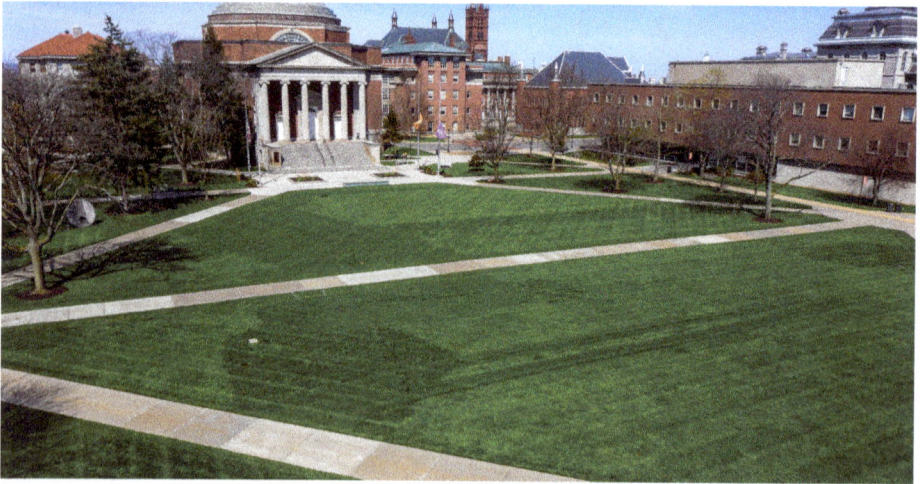

OKLAHOMA
University of Oklahoma Architecture Summer Academy

1-week (June) Residential Program – HS Students – Architecture, Interior Design, and Construction Science.

Design in Action: Creativity, Innovation, and Sustainability Shaping the Built Environment.

PENNSYLVANIA
Carnegie Mellon University Pre-College School of Architecture Program

4-, 6-week (July-August) Residential Program – HS Students – Intensive Studio Architecture Program

Explore interdisciplinary, contemporary practices; coursework includes analog drawing and digital media.

Seminars, workshops, portfolio development are included.

Chestnut Hill College Global Solutions Lab

Interactive Global Simulation, Electrifying Africa, & UN Sustainable Development Goals

1-week programs – HS Students – Intensive collaborative team solutions to big problems

Drexel University Westphal College of Media Arts & Design – Discovering Architecture

2-week Residential Program – HS Students – Intensive Studio Architecture Program

Visit prominent architectural, multi-disciplinary design offices; meet architects.

Maywood University Pre-College Summer Workshop School of Architecture

2-week (July) Residential Program – HS Students – Design Your Future Architecture Program.

Pennsylvania State University Pre-College AEspiring Architectural Engineering Camp

Five-day (June) camp for 9th grade to 12th grade.

Live in Penn State residence halls, eat at dining halls and at Berkey Creamery

Program artificial intelligence for construction purposes

Tour world-class labs and facilities with architects.

Temple University Tyler School of Art and Architecture Pre-College Architecture Program

Architecture Institute – Philadelphia, PA

2-week (July-August) Residential Program – HS Students – Studio Architecture Program.

RHODE ISLAND

Rhode Island School of Design Pre-College School of Architecture Program

6-week (June-July) Residential Program – HS Students – Foundational Art & Design Studies.

Figure drawing, projects, trips, exhibitions.

Roger Williams University High School Summer Academy in Architecture

4-week (July-August) Residential Program – Grades 11 & 12 – Explore Studio Architecture

Seminars, fieldwork, studio, portfolio development

SOUTH CAROLINA

Clemson University Pre-College School of Architecture Program

1-week (July-August) Residential Program – Grades 7-12

Engineering Design, Mechanical Engineering, Civil Engineering, Intelligent Vehicles, Materials Engineering.

TENNESSEE

The University of Memphis Discovering Architecture + Design

1-day – HS Students – Design programs on architecture, interior design, and the built environment.

The University of Tennesee, Knoxville College of Architecture + Design

1-week UT Summer Design Camp (July) Residential – HS Students

Immersive architecture, graphic design, and professional practice program.

TEXAS

Texas Tech Anson L Clark Scholars Program – Research Area: Architecture

7-week – Grades 11 & 12 – Residential Program (must be 17-years-old by start date) – no program fee

Intensive research-based program; $500 meal card; $750 tax-free stipend.

University of Houston & Wonderworks Pre-College Summer Discovery Program

Hines College of Architecture & Design – Introduction to Architecture

6-week – HS Students – Design programs with hands-on studio, field trips, and portfolio workshop.

The University of Texas at Austin Summer Design Camps – 2-D Game Design, 3-D Game Design, 3-D Animation/Motion

School of Design and Creative Technologies

1-week – HS Students – portfolio development and design.

VIRGINIA
Virginia Tech Inside Architecture + Design

1-week – HS Students – Hands-on design studio architecture program.

WISCONSIN
The University of Wisconsin Milwaukee School of Architecture & Urban Planning

1-week – HS Students – Design program on architecture, interior design, and the built environment.

CHAPTER 5

UNIVERSITY OPTIONS: WHAT COLLEGE PROGRAMS ARE THE BEST FOR ARCHITECTURE?

"Simplicity is the ultimate sophistication."

– Leonardo da Vinci

A s of March 2022, the National Architectural Accrediting Board (NAAB) included 181 accredited programs at 144 institutions. While not all of these schools are profiled in this book, you may find them at either the NAAB or the Association of Collegiate Schools of Architecture (ACSA).

The accredited programs offer one or more of the following degrees - B.Arch., M.Arch., and D.Arch.

There are 39 colleges offer both B.Arch. and M.Arch. degrees (or are candidates for both). There is one D.Arch. program.

There are five international NAAB accredited programs:
- American University in Dubai School of Architecture – B.Arch.
- American University of Sharjah School of Architecture and Design – B.Arch.
- Lebanese American University School of Architecture & Design – B.Arch.
- Universidad Peruana de Ciencias Aplicadas School of Architecture – B.Arch. (Candidate)
- Wenzhou-Kean University College of Architecture & Design – M.Arch. (Candidate)

ART, SCIENCE, MANAGEMENT

Architecture schools are embedded within the college of art, college of design, college of engineering, or college of architecture. Each university has a different title for the location in which its program is housed, though each program must satisfy a set of requirements embedded in the rules for accreditation. Though universities may offer different elective courses, they have essentially the same core classes.

Architecture studies intermix creativity and design with the analytical and technical aspects of building science and a large dose of project management and city planning. Spatial, environmental, and functional considerations must underly decision-making. Additional considerations include use, materials, logistics, and permits. Thus, architecture programs offer a holistic foundation for practical internship experiences and career development.

4-YEAR, 5-YEAR, 6-YEAR, 7-YEAR DEGREES

In looking through the profiles, you will see that some programs take four years, and some take longer. B.Arch. programs that lead to licensure are typically listed as 5-year programs, though the actual length of time varies.. Since some students arrive as first-year students with a significant number of college credits and AP units, the time-to-degree is not fixed. Some students finish their B.Arch. degree in four years. However, with the difficulty of classes, family challenges, or pressing problems, the program can also take longer.

Rice University, for example, offers a 6-year program where students earn their 4-year B.A. in Architecture, which is a more liberal arts-focused degree. Afterward, the student can continue to spend two additional years to earn the B.Arch. degree, which is focused on design science, construction, and management.

Typically, though, B.Arch. programs leading to licensure take five years while B.A. or B.S. in Architecture programs take four years. The path you take depends upon the certainty you have in your career goals. There is no right answer here because every person is different.

SELECTING COLLEGES

With different entrance requirements and different core concentrations, applicants must select a university that fits their academic profile, experience expectations, portfolio requirements, and design/technical abilities. Furthermore, not all architecture programs offer degrees leading to licensure. Colleges that offer the 4-year Bachelor of Arts in Architecture or Bachelor of Science in Architecture may have good programs with excellent studio spaces. However, you must earn a B.Arch. or M.Arch. to head down the road to licensure.

Some schools like Carnegie Mellon University offer both the 5-year B.Arch. licensure pathway degree, the 4-year Bachelor of Arts in Architecture, and a combination degree with another college within the university. In this situation you need to decide on your near-term goals. In the long run, if you decide not to complete the 5-year B.Arch., with a B.A. in Architecture, good grades, a strong portfolio, and references, you can pursue a M.Arch. degree if you choose to do so later.

At Harvard, for example, if you study architecture as an undergraduate, your 4-year degree is an A.B. in History of Art and Architecture, though if you have all of the requirements, grades, tests, experience, portfolio, recommendations, and are accepted, you can continue your education at Harvard in their M.Arch. degree program. Note that Harvard's M.Arch. program is seven semesters and a minimum of 140 units.

Northeastern's B.S. in Architecture is appealing for many reasons. However, the main reason is that you can complete your B.S. and then decide if you want to pursue licensure. If so, you are allowed to take one additional year to earn the M.Arch. While this may seem very similar to the example above with Harvard, the pathway from the B.S. to the M.Arch. degree at Northeastern is more assured and takes only one additional year. No doubt, the one year will be intensive, but this means that a student in Northeastern's program can earn a graduate M.Arch. degree in five years when other students are earning their undergraduate B.Arch. degree in the same amount of time.

Peripheral degrees might be another good option depending upon your interest. For example, Pratt Institute offers a B.A. in Construction Management, the University of Texas offers B.S. in Architectural Studies, B.S. Interior Design, and B.S. Architectural Engineering, and the University of Washington in Seattle offers a B.A. in Architectural Design. For something a little different, Miami University of Ohio offers a Bachelor of Fine Arts (B.F.A.) in Interior Design.

WHICH IS BEST?

Is the best college the one with the most prestigious undergraduate program? Is it the one with the best researchers, most publications, or the best teachers? Or, maybe, it is the one that has the most applicants, requires the highest test scores, or is ranked on a local or national list. Best is what you want in a school. Do you want large classes? Better facilities? Greater access to faculty? 24/7 studio time?

Some college's entrance requirements are extensive, and their acceptance rates are very low. Thus, for some schools like Harvard, MIT, Cornell, UPenn, Carnegie Mellon, and Wash U in St. Louis, you must be strategic with your planning to gain valuable training, develop your portfolio, and take the most challenging courses at your school.

The best college for you is the one that serves your needs. There are lists in the back of the book that organize schools in various ways along with some rankings.

If I were choosing an architecture school, I would want to attend a program with wildly brilliant, amazingly creative students who will become friends for life. I would want a studio space where I could work round-the-clock if I needed to and crash in a comfortable chair if I just could not keep my eyes open. I would want access to the gamut of fabrication equipment and materials. I would want engaging, dedicated, and talented professors who gave critiques but were not mean-spirited, overly critical, or derived joy in seeing students suffer. Trust me, I have more than 500-semester units and I have met them all. I would want a creative atmosphere where students encouraged each other and were awed and inspired to think differently. However, you are not me and you may have a different vision of college life.

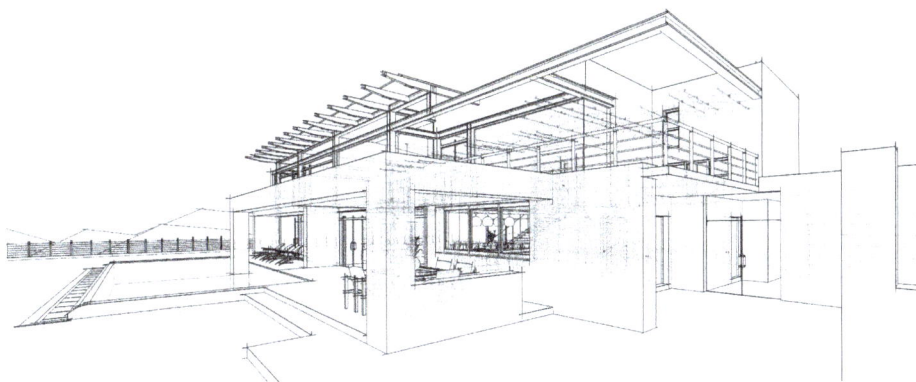

NATIONAL ARCHITECTURAL ACCREDITING BOARD (NAAB) OPTIONS

ALABAMA

Auburn Univ. – B.Arch.

Tuskegee Univ. – B.Arch.

ARIZONA

Arizona State Univ. – M.Arch.

Frank Lloyd Wright School of Arch. – M.Arch.

Univ. of Arizona – B.Arch., M.Arch.

ARKANSAS

Univ. of Arkansas – B.Arch.

CALIFORNIA

Academy of Art Univ. – B.Arch., M.Arch.

California Baptist Univ. – M.Arch.

California College of the Arts – B.Arch., M.Arch.

Cal Poly, Pomona - B.Arch., M.Arch.

Cal Poly, San Luis Obispo – B.Arch.

New School of Arch. & Design - B.Arch., M.Arch.

Southern CA Inst. of Arch. - B. Arch.; M. Arch.

UCLA – M.Arch.

Univ. of California, Berkeley – M.Arch.

USC - B.Arch.; M.Arch.

Woodbury Univ. - B.Arch., M.Arch.

COLORADO

Univ. of Colorado, Denver - M.Arch.

CONNECTICUT

Univ. of Hartford - M.Arch.

Yale Univ. - M.Arch.

DISTRICT OF COLUMBIA

Catholic Univ. - M.Arch.

Howard Univ. - B.Arch.

UDC - M.Arch.

FLORIDA

Florida A&M Univ. - B.Arch., M.Arch.

Florida Atlantic Univ. - B.Arch.

Florida Intl Univ. – M.Arch.

Univ. of Florida - M.Arch.

Univ. of Miami - B.Arch., M.Arch.

Univ. of South Florida - M.Arch.

GEORGIA

Georgia Tech - M.Arch.

Kennesaw State Univ. – B.Arch.

SCAD - M.Arch.

HAWAII

University of Hawaii, Manoa – D.Arch.

IDAHO

University of Idaho – M.Arch.

ILLINOIS

Illinois Inst. of Tech. – B.Arch., M.Arch.

Judson Univ. - M.Arch.

School of the Art Inst. of Chicago - M.Arch.

Southern Illinois Univ., Carbondale - M.Arch.

Univ. of Illinois, Chicago - M.Arch.

Univ. of Illinois, Urbana-Champaign - M.Arch.

INDIANA

Ball State Univ. - B.Arch., M.Arch.

Indiana Univ. - M.Arch. (Candidate)

Univ. of Notre Dame - B.Arch., M.Arch.

IOWA

Iowa State Univ. - B.Arch., M.Arch.

KANSAS

Kansas State Univ.- M.Arch.

Univ. of Kansas - M.Arch.

KENTUCKY

Univ. of Kentucky - M.Arch.

LOUISIANA

Louisiana Tech. Univ. - M.Arch.

Tulane University - B.Arch., M.Arch.

Univ. of Louisiana, Lafayette - M.Arch.

MAINE

Univ. of Maine, Augusta - B.Arch.

MARYLAND

Morgan State Univ. - M.Arch.

Univ. of Maryland - M.Arch.

MASSACHUSETTS

Boston Architectural College - B.Arch.,

M.Arch.

Harvard Univ. - M.Arch.

Massachusetts College of Art & Design - M.Arch.

MIT - M.Arch.

Northeastern Univ. - M.Arch.

Univ. of Massachusetts, Amherst - M.Arch.

Wentworth Inst. Of Tech. - M.Arch.

MICHIGAN

Andrews Univ. - M.Arch.

Ferris State - M.Arch.

Lawrence Technological Univ. - M.Arch.

Univ. of Detroit, Mercy - M.Arch.

Univ. of Michigan - M.Arch.

MINNESOTA

Dunwoody College of Tech. - B.Arch.

Univ. of Minnesota - M.Arch.

MISSISSIPPI

Mississippi State Univ. - B.Arch.

MISSOURI

Drury College - M.Arch.

Washington Univ., St. Louis - M.Arch.

MONTANA

Montana State Univ. M.Arch.

NEBRASKA

Univ. of Nebraska-Lincoln - M.Arch.

NEVADA

Univ. of Nevada, Las Vegas - M.Arch.

NEW JERSEY

Kean Univ. - M.Arch. (Candidate)

New Jersey Inst. Of Tech. - B.Arch., M.Arch.

Princeton Univ. - M.Arch.

NEW MEXICO

Univ. of New Mexico - M.Arch.

NEW YORK

City Univ. of New York - B.Arch., M.Arch.

Columbia Univ. - M.Arch.

Cooper Union - B.Arch.

Cornell Univ. - B.Arch., M.Arch.

N.Y.C. College of Tech. - B.Arch. (Candidate)

N.Y. Inst. Of Tech. - B.Arch., M.Arch. (Candidate)

Parsons School of Design - M.Arch.

Pratt Institute - B.Arch., M.Arch.

RPI - B.Arch., M.Arch.

RIT - M.Arch.

SUNY Buffalo - M.Arch.

SUNY at Alfred State - B.Arch.

Syracuse Univ. - B.Arch., M.Arch.

NORTH CAROLINA

North Carolina State Univ. - B.Arch., M.Arch.

NORTH DAKOTA

North Dakota State Univ. - M.Arch.

Univ. of North Carolina - B.Arch., M.Arch.

OHIO

Bowling Green State Univ. - M.Arch.

Kent State Univ. - M.Arch.

Miami Univ. - M.Arch.

Ohio State Univ. - M.Arch.

Univ. of Cincinnati - M.Arch.

OKLAHOMA

Oklahoma State Univ. - B.Arch.

Univ. of Oklahoma - B.Arch., M.Arch.

OREGON

Portland State Univ. - M.Arch.

Univ. of Oregon - B.Arch., M.Arch.

PENNSYLVANIA

Carnegie Mellon Univ. - B.Arch., M.Arch.

Drexel Univ. - B.Arch.

Marywood Univ. - B.Arch.

Penn State Univ. - B.Arch., M.Arch.

Philadelphia Univ. - B.Arch., M.Arch.

Temple Univ. - M.Arch.

UPenn - M.Arch.

PUERTO RICO

Polytechnic Univ. of Puerto Rico - B.Arch.

Pontifical Catholic Univ. - B.Arch.

Universidad Ana G. Mendez - M.Arch.

Universidad de Puerto Rico - M.Arch.

RHODE ISLAND

Rhode Island School of Design - B.Arch., M.Arch.

Roger Williams Univ. - M.Arch.

SOUTH CAROLINA

Clemson Univ. - M.Arch.

SOUTH DAKOTA

South Dakota State Univ. - M.Arch.

TENNESSEE

Belmont Univ. - B.Arch. (Candidate)

Univ. of Memphis - M.Arch.

Univ. of Tennessee, Knoxville - B.Arch., M.Arch.

TEXAS

Prairie View A&M Univ. - M.Arch.

Rice Univ. - B.Arch., M.Arch.

Texas A&M Univ. - M.Arch.

Texas Tech Univ. - M.Arch.

Univ. of Houston - B.Arch., M.Arch.

Univ. of Texas, Arlington - M.Arch.

Univ. of Texas, Austin - B.Arch., M.Arch.

Univ. of Texas, San Antonio - M.Arch.

UTAH

Univ. of Utah - M.Arch.

Utah Valley Univ. - B.Arch. (Candidate)

VERMONT

Norwich Univ. - M.Arch.

VIRGINIA

Hampton Univ. - M.Arch.

Univ. of Virginia - M.Arch.

Virginia Tech. - B.Arch., M.Arch.

WASHINGTON

Univ. of Washington - M.Arch.

Washington State Univ. - M.Arch.

WEST VIRGINIA

Fairmont State Univ. - M.Arch. (Candidate)

WISCONSIN

Univ. of Wisconsin, Milwaukee - M.Arch.

PRITZKER ARCHITECTURE PRIZE WINNERS

Established in 1979 to honor and recognize the top architects in the world, the Pritzker family's Hyatt Foundation grant what is often called "architecture's Nobel Prize". Winners are awarded $100,000 along with a bronze medallion. The following are the winners as of 2022.

2022 Laureate – *Diébédo Francis Kéré* (Born: Burkina Faso; Educated: Technical University of Berlin)

2021 Laureates – *Anne Lacaton* (Born: France; Educated: École nationale supérieure d'architecture et de paysage de Bordeaux; Master's in Urban Planning University of Bordeaux) **&** *Jean-Philippe Vassal* (Born: Morocco; Educated: École nationale supérieure d'architecture et de paysage de Bordeaux)

2020 Laureates – *Yvonne Farrell & Shelley McNamara* (BOTH - Born: Ireland; Educated: University College Dublin) (Born: Ireland; Educated: University College Dublin)

2019 Laureate – *Arata Isozaki* (Born: Japan; Educated: University of Tokyo – bachelor's and doctorate)

2018 Laureate – *B.V. Doshi* (Born: India; Educated: J.J. School of Architecture in Mumbai)

2017 Laureates – *Rafael Aranda*, *Carme Pigem*, & *Ramon Vilalta* (ALL – Born: Spain; Educated: Vallès School of Architecture)

2016 Laureate – *Alejandro Aravena* (Born: Chile; Educated Pontifical Catholic University of Chile and Università Iuav di Venezia)

2015 Laureate – Frei Otto

2014 Laureate – Shigeru Ban

2013 Laureate – Toyo Ito

2012 Laureate – Wang Shu

2011 Laureate – Eduardo Souto de Moura

2010 Laureates – Kazuyo Sejima and Ryue Nishizawa

2009 Laureate – Peter Zumthor

42

2008 Laureate – Jean Nouvel

2007 Laureate – Richard Rogers

2006 Laureate – Paulo Mendes da Rocha

2005 Laureate – Thom Mayne

2004 Laureate – Zaha Hadid

2003 Laureate – Jorn Utzon

2002 Laureate –Glenn Murcutt

2001 Laureates – Jacques Herzog and Pierre de Meuron

2000 Laureate – Rem Koolhaas

1999 Laureate – Norman Foster

1998 Laureate – Renzo Piano

1997 Laureate – Sverre Fehn

1996 Laureate – Rafael Moneo

1995 Laureate – Tadao Ando

1994 Laureate – Christian de Portzamparc

1993 Laureate – Fumihiko Maki

1992 Laureate – Alvaro Siza

1991 Laureate – Robert Venturi

1990 Laureate – Aldo Rossi

1989 Laureate – Frank Gehry

1988 Laureates – Gordon Bunshaft and Oscar Niemeyer

1987 Laureate – Kenzo Tange

1986 Laureate – Gottfried Bohm

1985 Laureate – Hans Hollein

1984 Laureate – Richard Meier

1983 Laureate – I.M. Pei

1982 Laureate – Kevin Roche

1981 Laureate – James Stirling

1980 Laureate – Luis Barragan

1979 Laureate – Philip Johnson

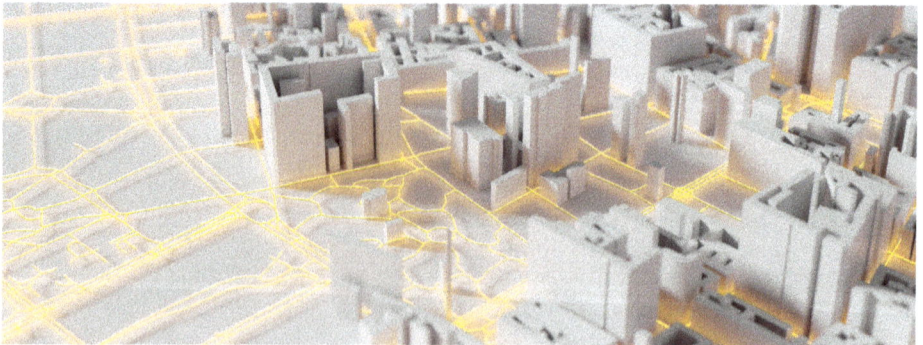

THE MANY ROADS TO ARCHITECTURE SUCCESS

Architecture belongs to culture, not to civilization.

- Alvar Alto

To be licensed in the United States and many other countries, you must undertake and finish a rigid set of requirements that take most people more than a decade to complete. Surprisingly some of the most famous architects in history did not graduate from college. Impatience, disenchantment, and frustration led some of the most brilliant minds in architecture history to drop out of college. The list of those who did not earn licensure in architecture includes,[1]

1. Frank Lloyd Wright
2. Louis Sullivan
3. Le Corbusier
4. Mies van der Rode
5. Buckminster Fuller
6. Luis Barragán
7. Carlo Scarpa
8. Tadao Ando
9. Peter Zumthor
10. Adolf Loos

FAMOUS N.Y.C. & D.C. BUILDINGS

NEW YORK CITY

Chrysler Building

> Architect: William Van Alen (Born: Brooklyn; Educated: Pratt Inst.)

Empire State Building

> Architect: William F. Lamb (Born: Brooklyn; Educated: Williams College, Columbia Univ, and Ecole des Beaux Arts)

Hearst Tower

> Architect: Norman Foster (Born: Stockport, England; Educated: Univ. of Manchester and Yale Univ.)

---

1   Suneet Zishan Langar, "9 Incredibly Famous Architects Who Didn't Possess an Architecture Degree," *ArchDaily*, June 19, 2017,https://www.archdaily.com/873850/9-incredibly-famous-architects-who-didnt-possess-an-architecture-degree

New York Times Building

> Renzo Piano (Born: Genoa, Italy; Educated: Univ. of Florence and Polytechnic Univ. of Milan)

One World Trade Center

> Architect: David Childs (Born: Princeton, NJ; Educated: Yale Univ.)

Rose Center for Earth & Space

> Architect: James Polshek (Born: Akron, OH; Educated: Case Western Reserve and Yale Univ.)

World Trade Center

> Architect: Minoru Yamasaki (Born: Seattle, WA; Educated: Univ. of Washington & NYU)

WASHINGTON, D.C.

Jefferson Memorial

> Architect: John Russell Pope (Born: NYC; Educated: Columbia Univ. and Ecole des Beaux Arts)

Ronald Reagan Building

> Architect: James Ingo Freed (Born: Essen, Germany; Educated: Illinois Institute of Technology)

Smithsonian National Air & Space Museum

> Architect: Gyo Obata (Born: S.F., CA; Educated: UC Berkeley and Wash U, St. Louis)

The White House

> Architect: James Hoban (Born: Ireland; Educated: National College of Art & Design)

Union Station

> Architect: Daniel Burnham (Born: Henderson, NY; Educated: N/A)

U.S. Supreme Court

> Architect: Cass Gilbert (Born: Zanesville, OH; Educated: Macalester College and MIT)

Vietnam Veterans Memorial

> Architect: Maya Lin (Born: Athens, OH; Educated: Yale Univ.)

Whatever college you attend, most of the road to success is in your effort, discipline, and vision. Many colleges will lead to your eventual goal. A few architecture greats did not earn a degree or licensure. Nevertheless, college is immensely valuable, though, and the only way to licensure. Lessons of all kinds are learned in your classes, studios, and internships. Enjoy each experience on your journey.

CHAPTER 6

WHAT IS THE DIFFERENCE BETWEEN A BA OR BS IN ARCHITECTURE, A B.ARCH., AND AN M.ARCH.?

"Architecture is the learned game, correct & magnificent, of forms assembled in the light."

– Le Corbusier

T here are 156 NAAB accredited and candidate architecture programs in 126 United States colleges.[1] There are nearly two hundred and fifty more that offer non-licensure architecture-related programs. Non-licensure architecture programs total 249 offered by 183 colleges. While some of these programs are housed in professional architecture departments, 74 programs in 69 colleges are unaffiliated.

Architecture is a ride – a physical ride and an intellectual ride.

– Antoine Predock

The following numbers of schools as of March 2022,[2]

Associate's + Certificate Undergraduate Programs

Architecture (non-licensure) A.A., A.S. + Certificate Programs = 30

Architecture, Engineering, Technology A.A., A.S. Programs = 240

Architectural Drafting A.A., A.S. + Certificate Programs = 253

Landscape Architecture A.A., A.S. + Certificate Programs = 10

Urban & Regional Planning A.A., A.S. + Certificate Programs = 5

Interior Architecture A.A., A.S. + Certificate Programs = 22

Art History A.A., A.S. + Certificate Programs = 7

Bachelor's + Candidate Degree Undergraduate Programs

NAAB Accredited Bachelor's Programs = 48

NAAB Accreditation Candidate Bachelor's Programs = 4

Architecture (non-licensure) Undergraduate Programs = 130

Architecture, Engineering, Technology (non-licensure) Undergraduate Programs = 54

Landscape Architecture Bachelor's Programs = 53

Urban & Regional Planning Bachelor's Programs = 41

Interior Architecture Bachelor's Programs = 37

Architectural History & Theory Bachelor's Programs = 12

Art History Bachelor's Programs = 392

1   ACSA, "Map of Programs," *ACSA*, July, 2014, https://www.acsa-arch.org/resource/nces-data-on-u-s-programs-in-architecture-and-related-fields/map-of-programs

2   Ibid.

Master's + Doctoral + Candidate Graduate Programs

NAAB Accredited Master's Programs = 102

NAAB Accreditation Candidate Master's Programs = 8

NAAB Accredited Doctoral Programs = 1

Architecture (non-licensure) Graduate Programs = 84

Architecture, Engineering, Technology (non-licensure) Graduate Programs = 17

Landscape Architecture Master's + Doctoral Programs = 59

Urban & Regional Planning Master's + Doctoral Programs = 99

Interior Architecture Master's + Doctoral Programs = 13

Real Estate Development Master's + Doctoral Programs = 8

Architectural History & Theory Master's + Doctoral Programs = 10

Art History Master's + Doctoral Programs = 117

UNDERGRADUATE AND GRADUATE DEGREES

AA – Associate of Arts: 2-year degree

AS – Associate of Science: 2-year degree

BA – Bachelor of Arts: 4-year degree

BS – Bachelor of Science: 4-year degree

BFA – Bachelor of Fine Arts – 4-year degree

B.F.A. Arch. – Bachelor of Fine Arts in Architecture – 4-, 5-year degree

B.Arch. – Bachelor of Architecture – 5-, 6-year degree

B.Envd. or B.E.D. – Bachelor of Environmental Design

M.A. – Master of Arts – 1-3-year degree earned after the BA, BS, BFA, or B.Arch.

M.S. – Master of Science – 1-3-year degree earned after the BA, BS, BFA, or B.Arch.

M.Arch. – Master of Architecture – 1-4-year degree earned after the BA, BS, BFA, or B.Arch.

MLA – Master of Landscape Architecture – 1-3-year degree earned after the BA, BS, BFA, or B.Arch.

MFA – Master of Fine Arts – 1-3-year degree earned after the BA, BS, BFA, or B.Arch.

THE SEVEN MAJOR DIFFERENCES BETWEEN THE ASSOCIATE, BACHELOR'S, AND MASTER'S DEGREES

1. Starting Point
2. Academic Discipline
3. Time to Completion
4. Location of the Education
5. Educational Costs
6. Earning Power
7. Professional Opportunities

STARTING POINT

Most students who begin by earning an Associate of Arts (AA) or Associate of Science (AS) have no college credits. Starting their college education from scratch, they accumulate units to transfer. Most complete 60+ units, typically at a community college. While students can earn AA or AS degrees at a community college, some earn this degree at a 4-year college or university. The AA or AS is either a terminal degree, meaning that the student will not continue on with their bachelor's degree or just a stepping stone to their BA, BS, BFA, BFA Arch., or B.Arch. The difference between the associate's and bachelor's degrees is just the starting point.

The starting point for students who pursue a bachelor's degree may be farther along the traditional 4-year pathway. Meanwhile, the starting point for the master's degree (MA, MS, MFA, MLA, or M.Arch.) begins after obtaining a bachelor's degree.

ACADEMIC DISCIPLINE

Every degree encompasses different requirements. Courses for the Associate of Science (AS) may differ from an Associate of Arts (AA), particularly for math and science classes. Similarly, the requirements for the BA, BS, BFA, BFA Arch., and B.Arch. also differ. With two or more additional years of coursework, the BA, BS, BFA, BFA Arch., and B.Arch. are more thorough. The MA, MS, MFA, MLA, M.Arch., and D.Arch. build upon the bachelor's degree. Architecture students will not take the same classes as those studying architectural history. Even so, a few may overlap. Though the essential skills for each career area are distinct, course requirements are often also unique. Furthermore, with the myriad of combinations, it is rare that any two undergraduate students have the same classes in the same exact order.

TIME TO COMPLETION

AA and AS degrees typically take two years, while most BA, BS, BFA, BFA Arch., and B.Arch. degrees are 4-,5-, and 6-year programs, depending upon full-time or part-time status. Students who transfer in credits or earn credits otherwise can reduce their time to completion. Some students may choose to extend their education with a minor or by earning a second bachelor's degree in another field. By cross-training, students open more doors. Additionally, a degree in business on the bachelor's level or Master's in Business Administration (MBA) may lead to alternative leadership positions. Time in college can be reduced.

Some students enter a BA, BS, BFA, BFA Arch., and B.Arch. program having already completed college credits because they were dual-enrolled or they took college classes directly through a college or university ahead of time. Some high school students take AP/ IB tests after completing higher-level courses. By earning qualifying scores, colleges and universities sometimes grant transferrable credits.

Other ways students can enter at different starting points include credit-by-exam, CLEP tests, experiential credits, and those granted in the military. Colleges and universities are keenly aware of the challenges students face today with work, illness, and family responsibilities. Thus, many schools of higher education offer flexible enrollment with opportunities for part-time, evening, weekend, and online classes.

LOCATION OF THE EDUCATION

The AA and AS are earned at colleges that grant 2-year degrees. The location may be at a local community college or a university. BA, BS, BFA, BFA Arch., and B.Arch. programs are offered at a 4-year college or university. However, with online classes, students have the flexibility to take classes anywhere. Thus, the location in which a typical student studies is not set in stone. Nevertheless, since studios are fixed, challenges need to be overcome in getting support and feedback which may be easier in person.

EDUCATIONAL COSTS

Since the AA or AS requires a shorter amount of time and is typically completed at a lower-cost community college, the cost for an associate's degree is typically less than a bachelor's degree. Master's degree programs cost more per credit but take less time than a bachelor's degree. On the other hand, many students can obtain financial aid in the form of grants, loans, and both merit and need-based scholarships. This aid can pay for school and reduce debt after college.

EARNING POWER

Students with more education can earn more. According to National Center for Educational Statistics (NCES) data, on average, the more education a person has the higher salary they can command. Of course, there is a wide range in annual salaries from those who have consistent projects and are paid six-digit or seven-digit incomes to those who have very few contracts. Thus, there is great variation.

PROFESSIONAL OPPORTUNITIES

Earning a BA, BS, BFA, BFA Arch., or B.Arch. opens more doors than an AA or AS. Similarly, an MA, MS, MFA, MLA, or M.Arch. often opens more doors than a bachelor's degree. B.Arch. and M.Arch. degrees require more training than traditional bachelor's and master's degrees. You can also obtain additional training through workshops or studio classes. With a scholarship to pay for college, you might find that the training and opportunities are worth your time. Besides, you will gain additional skills that could prove valuable in your future.

Live in the present and make it so beautiful that it's worth remembering.

– Arnold H. Glasow

2-YEAR AND 4-YEAR UNDERGRADUATE
SKILL DEVELOPMENT & LIBERAL ARTS DEGREES

Basically, BA and BS degrees are degrees that typically offer a liberal arts foundation along with a major or concentration in a specific subject. Meanwhile, a BFA is considered a professional arts-focused degree with fewer courses in English, science, math, social science, and the humanities. Thus, the BFA is a specialist qualification in the arts and is more focused on the specific area of art you choose.

The BA and BS degrees include significantly more liberal arts classes and thus are more general degrees. However, the intention of the BFA degree is for students to pursue an arts-focused curriculum, and thus there are fewer general subject courses.

Finally, while many AA or AS degrees are focused on providing initial technical or professional skills, an AA or AS in these areas are often interchangeable. Similarly, a BA or BS in architecture degrees are often interchangeable. However, a BFA may be seen as different since there is typically more coursework focused on specific arts pursuits, and thus, you may have more technical experiences and knowledge than someone who has a BA or BS.

ROAD TO LICENSURE - B.ARCH. OR M.ARCH.

The direction you head with your career goals may change with new insights and opportunities that unfold as you begin your course of study. Heading toward a college architecture program requires asking yourself the first major question. Do you want to earn a B.Arch. (Bachelor of Architecture), which is typically a 5-year program leading to licensure, or do you want to pursue a 4-year B.A. or B.S. program in architecture?

If you are unsure if architecture is right for you but you believe the art, design, science, and technology focus fits your overall interest, the B.A. or B.S. in Architecture may be the right choice. Another avenue is to head toward urban planning, construction, building science, industrial design, interior architecture, or landscape design. Afterward, you can always attend graduate school to earn your M.Arch. (Master of Architecture). The B.A. or B.S. offers a more liberal arts approach and will have some studio classes as well.

While most architecture programs Include studio and design classes, the B.A. or B.S. frequently offers more theory, history, and sociology. If you want to pursue licensure, you will need to continue with further study in an M.Arch. program if you want to practice as an architect. Some M.Arch. programs require one year of study while others take two, three, or four. To enter an M.Arch. program, students must have completed a bachelor's degree as well as all additional prerequisites for the graduate school in which they plan to attend.

The B.Arch. or the M.Arch. must be accredited through the National Architectural Accrediting Board. After earning the B.Arch. or M.Arch., prospective architects must pass the Architect Registration Examination (ARE) and complete the qualification process to become an architect. The six steps are:

1. Earn a B.Arch. or M.Arch. degree
   - Comparable degrees are possible in some cases
2. Set up an active National Council of Architectural Registration Boards (NCARB) Record
   - Select a jurisdiction
   - Receive eligibility to test from that board

3. Gain Field Experience
    - Architectural Experience Program (AXP)
        o 3,740 supervised field hours required
        o At least half must be supervised under an architect
    - Comparable experience options are possible
    - Document experience in an AXP Portfolio
    - Identify your architect supervisor
4. Pass the Architect Registration Exam (ARE 5.0) – 6 parts/sections/divisions
    - Practice Management
    - Project Management
    - Programming & Analysis
    - Project Planning & Design
    - Project Development & Documentation
    - Construction & Evaluation
5. The Rolling Clock
    - After you pass an ARE 5.0 division, your score remains valid within a 5-year window
    - Once you complete all divisions, none of your divisions will expire.
    - The rolling clock can be extended in extenuating circumstances
6. Apply for State-Level Licensure
    - Requirements vary by state

ARE 5.0 PASS RATES BY SECTION

Division	2018	2019	2020	2021
Practice Management	51%	49%	51%	53%
Project Management	62%	63%	63%	63%
Programming & Analysis	53%	52%	50%	52%
Project Planning & Design	46%	42%	45%	47%
Project Development & Documentation	53%	50%	57%	53%
Construction & Evaluation	70%	70%	66%	62%
Number of Candidates Testing	15,493	18,605	13,464	16,173

You will need to choose the jurisdiction in which you would like to receive your license. Each state or jurisdiction may have different requirements. The Architect Registration Exam (ARE) is focused on professionalism in the areas of health, safety,

and welfare. Competencies include:
- Architectural Business Practices
- Legal, Ethical, and Contractual Standards
- Coordinating Project Team Activities
- Programmatic and Regulatory Requirements
- Design Alternatives
- Appropriate Materials and Building Systems
- Project Documentation
- Construction Phase Services
- Project Assessment
- Environmental Sustainability, Resiliency, and Adaptation

The license is accepted by 55 NCARB jurisdictions and Canada. The 55 jurisdiction include 50 states, the District of Columbia, Puerto Rico, Guam, the Northern Mariana Islands, and the U.S. Virgin Islands. While this designation is general, each state has its own set of requirements to practice.

The National Council of Architectural Registration Boards (NCARB) serves as the overseer of licensure in the fifty-five U.S. states and territories. NCARB's centralized hub (1) facilitates licensure, (2) fosters collaboration, and (3) centralizes data for all licensing boards.

Whether you are considering the licensure route by earning a B.Arch. or pursuing a B.S. or B.A. in Architecture, you should plan so you are prepared. Most schools want undergraduate applicants to have AP or college calculus and AP or college physics before entry. These two classes are nearly non-negotiable given the amount of engineering design required in studio classes. However, at the same time, artistry is also imperative.

Whichever program you choose make sure you learn and enhance the analytical, technical, communication, management, and organization skills you need. Combined with your imagination, creativity, and vision, you will be set whichever dIrection you choose.

The world always seems brighter when you've just made something that wasn't there before.

– Neil Gaiman

CHAPTER 7

COLLEGE ADMISSIONS: APPLICATIONS, ESSAYS, RECOMMENDATIONS, AND FINANCIAL AID

"Architecture is the stage on which we live our lives."

– Mariam Kamara

With amazing faculty, excellent facilities, and easy access to internships, Pratt Institute and Cooper Union stand out as two of the premier schools for architecture. Both offer a rigorous course of study and socially responsible projects on the cutting edge of design and technology.

Pratt Institute offers a 5-year B.Arch., B.S. in Construction Management, M.Arch., and M.S. in Architecture. Notable alumni include some of the best in the world, including

- William Van Alen, an American architect who designed New York City's Chrysler Building
- Peter Zumthor, a Swiss architect who won the Pritzker Prize in 2009
- Carlos Zapata, an American architect who worked on the Cooper Square Hotel in Manhattan, Concourse J at Miami International Airport, and the Bitexco Financial Tower in Ho Chi Minh City.

Cooper Union offers a 5-year B.Arch. and an M.S. in Architecture. The university also has an impressive list of notable architecture graduates including

- Chuck Hoberman, an inventor, architect, and engineer known for inventing folding structures – most notably the Hoberman sphere.
- David Heymann, an American architect that was commissioned by former President George W. Bush to design an eco-friendly building.

SCHOLARSHIPS

Nearly every university in the United States offers need-based scholarships. You apply for these by submitting the Free Application for Federal Student Aid (FAFSA) found at *www.studentaid.gov* and sometimes also the College Scholarship Service (CSS) Profile through the College Board website at *www.collegeboard.org*

Additionally, most colleges also offer merit scholarships. Many are listed in the profile section. Check it out. Below are a couple of schools chosen at random to give you a sense of a few of the options listed in the profile section.

Auburn University

Auburn University, including its College of Architecture, Design, and Construction, awards approximately $200,000 in scholarships each year. Submission of the FAFSA is not required for merit scholarships, though it is recommended.

Cornell University

Cornell offers nine scholarships each year specifically for architecture students. Additionally, Cornell offers its Future Architect Award for underrepresented students.

Harvard University

While Harvard does not offer specific awards for architecture students, students whose families earn less than $65,000 pay no tuition.

Illinois Institute of Technology

IIT offers some valuable architecture scholarships, including the Crown Scholarships, which provide full tuition for five years. There are also undergraduate merit scholarships including the full 5-year Camras Scholarship and the Duchossois Leadership Scholarship which includes 5-year tuition + room & board.

Savannah College of Art and Design (SCAD)

Some colleges are exceptionally generous with money for a large proportion of students. At SCAD, 80% of new applicants receive merit & need-based scholarships. This includes U.S. citizens, permanent residents, and international students.

Washington University in St. Louis

Wash U offers scholarships as well. However, while some schools, like Texas A&M, consider all undergraduate and graduate College of Architecture students for scholarships, some of Wash U's scholarships require additional applications. Wash U offers one full scholarship and up to five additional $10,000 annual scholarships. Look at the James W. Fitzgibbon Scholarship in Architecture, which requires a digital portfolio and additional merit-based scholarships like the Danforth Scholars, Annika Rodriguez Scholars, and John B. Ervin Scholars.

COLLEGE ADMISSIONS:

Success in the Face of Uncertainty

There are no guarantees in college admissions. However, planning is essential for success. The most beneficial advice is to pursue your passions with gusto, train to be the best you can be, take advantage of internships and experiences, and meet lots of people along the way.

Remember, "life is a journey, not a destination." Often the journey is more exciting, leading to lessons, friendships, and indelible moments. However, the fact is…in the end, if college is your goal, then you need to remember a few action items to be successful.

Should you worry about grades? Of course. You should also take classes that will challenge you. Colleges pick the best candidates from those who apply. Students must be academically prepared, socially conscious, and talented in a few different areas in which they are passionate (design, graphic arts, musical instruments, theatre, debate, public speaking, leadership, athletics, community service, computer coding, robotics, construction, etc.).

The college selection process is not that much different than companies picking employees. While colleges are more or less competitive, companies may have only one job and a hundred resumes. Discover the unique drive and internal motivations within you that make you the very best you can be. Be exceptional at what you choose to do academically, personally, and professionally.

Most of all, You Do You

TALENT FOCUSED

Not all schools require high grades and test scores. Many are simply interested in selecting students who are the most talented, most driven, and the most willing to be team players on the college campus. Thus, while you should take a solid set of courses and fulfill requirements, only the top schools emphasize completing a challenging curriculum, high grades, and standardized test scores.

FOR HIGHLY SELECTIVE COLLEGES, TALENT IS JUST THE BEGINNING

A few highly selective colleges seek extraordinary talent over academics, but most zero in on a student's challenging courses and high grades. To gain admission into the most highly selective colleges, you must take the most challenging course load you can manage and succeed. Highly selective colleges want disciplined scholars AND remarkably talented students.

Determine what you can handle, knowing that some colleges with extremely competitive admission will only take students who have completed more than ten AP, IB, or honors classes over the four years, including AP Calculus BC and AP Physics C. AP Statistics and AP Environmental Science, are not of equal rigor in their eyes.

Why would these most competitive colleges require these classes? However daunting these classes may seem, remember, the top colleges have lots of applicants and they need to draw the line somewhere. UCLA had 149,779 applicants for fall 2022 and UC Berkeley had 128,192 applicants. The numbers are truly staggering since neither freshman class will not have more than 7,000 freshmen starting in the fall.

College admissions can feel like a rollercoaster of energy and emotion. Creating a portfolio of talent, training, and experience is just the beginning. Meanwhile, some colleges want to see standardized test scores which are aided by practice. Applications and essays may seem easy at first but managing the various requirements and deadlines can be difficult. Therefore, this moment is a good time to get a calendar and organize your tasks.

REQUEST INFORMATION

Almost every college has a location, a link, or a contact us page where you can request information from the school. If you are considering a school, request information from them. In this way, they may send you updates, scholarship opportunities, a valuable application fee waiver, special invites, and other information that could be valuable in the process. Of course, you may not need one more e-mail, and you may be receiving e-mails from the school anyway. Still, I recommend that you fill out their form. Then, since you are likely to be inundated with e-mails, make a folder to the left of your e-mail in-box for colleges you are considering. Then, when you get an e-mail from one of those schools, file it away.

STANDARDIZED TESTING

A few schools still require standardized testing. Check first. Many colleges are test-optional. This means that you are not required to take the SAT or ACT. However, if you do have a good score, it may make all the difference in gaining admission. College admissions offices are studying this topic and considering their future policies. Much of their concern began with test cancelations worldwide due to the pandemic.

Test centers did not want to let students into their site to take the test who may be infected, nor were they able to ensure safety. In addition, social distancing requirements limited the number of students who could take a test at any given site. Yet, for decades, college admissions decisions centered around grades and test scores. This change in the landscape of decision-making has rattled admissions departments.

Meanwhile, some colleges proclaim that test-optional truly means that the tests are not required. Yet, evidence proves otherwise. Thus, many students are still taking the test and working around the hurdles amid the confusion. Competition continues to drive students to present evidence to show that they are worthy candidates. In the end, colleges need to make a final decision between very good applicants. If one student has a high score, that student may have a higher likelihood of admission depending upon the admissions committee's decision-making process.

Data show that students who submitted scores within the college's range or higher were accepted at a higher rate than those without a score. Also, it stands to reason that if students with low scores did not submit and only those with high scores did, the college-documented average SAT and ACT score will necessarily increase.

Some schools are test blind in that they say that they do not consider your scores. A few of these colleges still provide a place for you to input your scores, thus, they are not truly blind. Nevertheless, the decision regarding whether you take the test or submit the score is yours. If the school does not require an admissions test, then you can choose to take the test and submit it as you like. If your academics are solid and you are willing to prepare for the test, you should take the test.

APPLYING EARLY

Early Action (EA), Restricted Early Action (REA), and Early Decision (ED)

With low acceptance rates, the chance to get more scholarship money, and chaos surrounding the cancellations and changes in AP, IB, SAT, and ACT testing, students clamor to apply early to schools. In addition, applications to top schools increased during the pandemic, resulting in colleges making difficult admissions decisions in their quest to build a diverse, talented, and engaged class of students. Furthermore, students applying early have access to many more scholarship options. This confluence sent students in droves to apply early and this trend is likely to continue.

In Early Action (EA), Restricted Early Action (REA), and Early Decision (ED), students apply in late summer or early fall to college and generally find out around winter break, though some decisions come out earlier and a few arrive later. This advantage not only gives students the chance for more scholarship money in some cases but the benefit of finding out early reduces the tension of the long waiting period to find out about Regular Decision schools.

Early Action (EA) and Restricted Early Action (REA) are different. In restricted early action, a limitation is placed on either how many or what colleges you can apply to simultaneously. Many REA schools do not allow students to apply to other early action schools, though some will allow students to apply early to public colleges. Check the colleges to be sure. In addition, some schools like Georgetown will allow students to apply EA elsewhere but not apply to a binding Early Decision (ED) program where the student commits to attending if they are accepted. However, most EA schools do not have these restrictions, and some students apply to a handful of EA schools during the admissions process.

Early Decision (ED) is a binding agreement between the student and college with signatures from the student's parents and the high school assuring that the student is committed and will attend. Each of these parties acknowledges and agrees that, if granted admission, they will fulfill their agreement. There are caveats to this, though you should go into the agreement fully committing to your ED school. This must be your top choice school.

There are incentives to applying ED. Frequently, acceptance rates are higher with ED. Also, at some schools, a large percentage of their class is filled with students who profess their unequivocal love for their dream school. Students who know they have a top choice school, have the necessary admissions prerequisites fulfilled, and are committed to accepting the binding agreement to attend, should apply ED.

COMMON APPLICATION, COALITION APPLICATION, OR COLLEGE-SPECIFIC APPLICATION

Every college's process is unique. However, there are a few commonalities. In 2022, approximately 900 colleges used the Common App; about 150 colleges used the Coalition Application. A few used both. The University of California system has its own application as do the California State Universities and the Texas schools.

The Common App and Coalition App may be started early. In your junior year, consider getting a head start on reviewing what is required. The college-specific questions may change each year. However, the basic application is generally the same and can be created ahead of time. At the end of July, make a copy of everything you have completed just in case.

Some schools admit on a rolling basis. 'Rolling' means that periodically, after all of the materials are received, the admissions committee determines who they will accept, and they send the notification right away. Many students are accepted as early as August. The thrill of acceptance cannot be overstated.

ESSAYS

The Common Application and Coalition essays are often posted months ahead of time. Since this main essay is required or recommended for nearly all of the Common Application and Coalition Application schools, this is a good place to start thinking about what you might want to say to colleges.

In addition to the main essay on the Common Application and Coalition Application, about three-fours of the colleges have their own specific questions or essays. In August, most admissions applications are open and ready for you to dive into the college-specific questions, though many of the essays are available earlier and some schools hold out until later for their big essay reveal.

These can be prepared ahead of time too. One popular question is, "What activity is most important to you and why?" Another is "Why did you choose your major?" A third common question is, "Why do you want to attend our school?" Other essays you should prepare, or at least consider, surround the topics of diversity, adversity, and challenges. Everyone has a challenge they needed to overcome. What did you learn from that experience?

Complete the application fully. Think carefully about optional sections. Typically, universities offer you the chance to provide the school with just the right cherry on top of the ice cream sundae expressing something about you that is unique. If you have absolutely nothing to say, then leave it blank. There is also an additional information section on the main Common App, Coalition Application, and University of California application. This is not a place to write another essay, but you can put information that could not be adequately explained on the rest of the application.

There are also some schools that include scholarship essays within the supplement part of the application. Start early.

LETTERS OF RECOMMENDATION

Most colleges, though not all, request letters of recommendation from a counselor and one or more teachers. For B.Arch. programs, the university may want not only mathematics and science teachers but an art teacher as well. Plan for this. Occasionally, there is a section for optional recommendations too. In this location, you might get a recommendation from a summer program leader or someone with whom you did an internship. If you were in a sport, there is a location for a coach on about a quarter of the applications. Finally, if there is a supplemental application, for example on SlideRoom, these often require separate recommendations reviewed by the architecture program.

DECISIONS, DECISIONS: WAITING FOR A RESPONSE

The period between submitting your application and getting your admissions results may not require a tremendous amount of work, but it does require patience and diligence. First, most schools will send you a link to a portal where you will check your results, though the most important reason for checking every couple of weeks is to ensure that the college is not missing something or has not offered you the chance to apply for an extra scholarship.

Check your portal regularly. Otherwise, read the college's correspondence sent through your e-mail. Waiting is difficult. These few months are a tough period of time because students want to know. However, on the portal, the college typically lists the date they will send out the results. Other popular sites post college admission notifications too. You will find out soon.

CELEBRATING ACCEPTANCES AND DEALING WITH REJECTION

Acceptance is not guaranteed. The probabilities are low at the most highly selective schools. However, you just need to work hard in school to have what it takes and give this commitment to academics all you have. When you find out the results, you will celebrate your acceptances.

Congratulations! The colleges in which you gain admission go on your list of wins. Check your financial aid and scholarship packages too. Money is often an important factor in making your decision. Consider visiting the school. Many students apply to college merely by someone's recommendation, *U.S. News and World Report* ranking, looking at campus photos on Google, or researching profiles posted on a website or in a book.

There is nothing that replaces the actual campus visit. After all, you will be spending a few years there. While you may not be accepted everywhere you apply, you may decide when you visit that the college is high on your list or that you do not want to apply after all. The pandemic's uncertainty added more question marks to an already complicated set of admissions processes.

The buzzword for 2020-2030 is resilience. It is never easy to be rejected. However, rejection happens. You will survive. Note that many colleges still accept applications in April, May, and June long after most school's applications are closed. Look up those colleges if you did not get accepted or if you want to see what other schools might be good options for you. In April and May, Google

"College Openings Update". You will be surprised to see the colleges that show up on the list that still have open spots.

WAITLISTS: THE ART OF WAITING

Confirm immediately if you are given a waitlist spot and still want to attend. There is often a deadline. You do not want to miss the date. If you are no longer interested or have selected another school, go into the portal and turn down the offer. Someone else is bound to be thrilled by your anonymous "gift".

Next, if you are still highly interested, find the location on the portal or site designated by the college to update them on what you have done – accomplishments, awards, extra class, honors, art, shows, or films. You only want to add what they have not yet seen, but if you have taken the initiative to do something more than what you originally stated on the application, by all means, tell them.

You could just wait for their decision, but you are better off being proactive and showing that you really want to be at their school. Students do get off of the waitlists at most schools. How much do you want to attend? Meanwhile, you will have to deposit somewhere else before the May 1st deadline. Stay hopeful. This next year will be a significant step along your journey. Relax!

CHAPTER 8

SUPPLEMENTAL MATERIALS AND PORTFOLIOS FOR ARCHITECTURE PROGRAMS

"For the most part things never get built the way they were drawn."

– Maya Lin

At the top schools like Cornell University, Washington University in St. Louis, Carnegie Mellon, MIT, and Harvard, acceptance is very difficult. The B.Arch. degree is one of the most intense and most demanding degrees students can earn in college. Mastering design, engineering, and technology in individual and collaborative projects is challenging. Students must be on the ball, multitalented, and extremely focused.

Students must be literally and figuratively brilliant and unstoppable. With that kind of multitasking intensity and vigorous competition, admissions officers and program directors are as interested in the applicant's analytical ability as they are in their talent. As a result, after a portfolio review, many student candidates will interview, demonstrating their commitment to architecture and their potential.

CHANGES IN THE APPLICANT DEMOGRAPHICS
CHALLENGES ON THE ROAD AHEAD

COVID-19 shook students as well as admissions offices. Particularly in studio-centered majors, when colleges closed down or went online, they lost many students in their programs. International students left for their country of origin and classes at a distance could not provide the needed materials and opportunities. Many quit and did not return.

Furthermore, some architecture programs completely shut down. The field faced a crisis. While some programs reopened after COVID-19, and some students returned, demographic shifts changed the dynamics, including gender diversity and ethnic makeup. The decreased population of international students shook architecture programs. Nevertheless, there are still many students applying.

Other challenges existed as well. COVID-19 changed the types of applicants to college. Many students of color did not apply. Even when African American and Hispanic students completed their programs, they did not achieve licensure at the same rate as other students. Meanwhile, other data show that while enrollments rebounded, some programs had budget cuts.

ARCHITECTURE ADMISSIONS

While many architecture programs only have about a couple of dozen students, Cal Poly San Luis Obispo has one of the largest programs with about 850 attendees. Twenty percent of all architects in California and five percent of architects in the entire U.S. are Cal Poly graduates. Cal Poly's program is intense, but there are perks like connections to architecture firms, current technology, large studios, and dedicated exhibition space. Yet, even with such a large program, gaining admissions is very competitive, particularly since there is no portfolio requirement.

Furthermore, Cal Poly dissuades students from changing majors into their program. To change into architecture students must (1) finish a quarter, (2) complete calculus, (3) make a one chance request, (4) and satisfy a list of protocols and requirements. Since Cal Poly's program is impacted, applying in one major and changing into architecture is discouraged. However, these stipulations are not as rigid at all colleges, and outstanding students can transfer into architecture given a strong academic record, prerequisites completed, and the demonstration of ability, interest, talent, and fortitude.

The admissions process can seem daunting. Portfolios are required at many colleges. Since students often apply to 10-20 schools, some become overwhelmed if they do not start early. Applying and portfolio development takes a ton of dedicated time and money for training, preparation, application fees, and other expenses.

Since a B.Arch. is necessary for licensure, students must be disciplined and ready for the demanding program of study. However, if you have a hunger to pursue architecture and train for your passion, commitment, and desire, you could reach and exceed your goals. The knowledge you acquire by studying architecture may also come in handy if you change your major. You only have to read a few blogs or threads to grasp the stories of students who discussed their journey, overcame hurdles, found their niche, or decided their pathway in architecture. As Euclid once said, "There is no royal road." The journey from trainee to architecture takes mental and physical stamina with ups and downs. Even so, anything is possible.

PORTFOLIO REQUIREMENTS

The first entry point to architecture is your college application and admission to the program. You may not get accepted to your dream school. Even so, you might find that another school that did accept you is a perfect fit. One of my students with very high grades and test scores, completed Cornell's summer program, her school's engineering magnet program, and won awards for art but was not accepted into Cornell. However, she is now at MIT. She often says that she cannot imagine going anywhere else. Although MIT does not have a B.Arch. program and Cornell does, she had a dozen other excellent choices and is completing her B.S. in Architecture at MIT and plans to earn her M.Arch. at MIT or another university. So, let's look at the portfolio requirements at a few schools.

Some programs do not accept a portfolio like Cal Poly, Texas A&M, UT Austin, and Auburn. However, others do not require a portfolio but art pieces are reviewed. Colleges that consider these optional submissions include Southern California Institute of Architecture, Georgia Tech, MIT, and Harvard University. The requirements for a few schools are listed below.

CARNEGIE MELLON UNIVERSITY

5-year Bachelor of Architecture (B.Arch.),
4-year Bachelor of Arts in Architecture (B.A.),
4-year BXA Intercollege Degree

All three of CMU's architecture programs require a SlideRoom portfolio. Applicants begin the process by applying to CMU and answering the college-specific questions (College of Fine Arts; School of Architecture). From the link on the application or directly into SlideRoom, log in, complete the questions and submit the required materials. These include 2 forms; 10 creative works. Register to participate in an online, formal, one-on-one portfolio review with a faculty member via Zoom. This is available in SlideRoom. While not required, this faculty interview and portfolio review is strongly recommended.

CORNELL UNIVERSITY

5-year Bachelor of Architecture (B.Arch.)

Students applying to Cornell must apply through the Common Application. Prospective B.Arch. students must request a portfolio interview with a professor or alumna with artwork samples. Students will submit portfolios via SlideRoom with 15-20 slides and carefully crafted captions. Submissions should include freehand drawings and a range of artistic media.

PRATT INSTITUTE

5-year Bachelor of Architecture (B.Arch.)

After completing the Common Application, students will submit a SlideRoom supplement. Media uploads can include images, video, 3D models, audio, or documents. You can submit your resume as a media upload, in the additional notes field on SlideRoom, or on your status portal after submission. The SlideRoom submission will not be read by admissions, just the arts faculty.

RHODE ISLAND SCHOOL OF DESIGN

5-year Bachelor of Architecture (B.Arch.)

After completing the Common Application, students will submit a SlideRoom supplement. Students present 12-20 of their recent work on the SlideRoom site. RISD requests finished pieces, drawings from direct observation, and no more than three pieces that show research and prep work. RISD's admissions are competitive so you should curate and edit the pieces you choose to submit in your portfolio.

CHAPTER 9

POST PANDEMIC EMPLOYMENT OUTLOOK: STATISTICS AND ECONOMIC PROJECTIONS

"Architecture should speak of its time and place, but yearn for timelessness."

– Frank Gehry

Architects play essential roles. According to the *Occupational Outlook Handbook*, employment opportunities in architecture and engineering are slated to grow 6% from 2020 to 2030 with approximately 146,000 new jobs expected. The median annual wage for entry-level positions was $83,160. Since rebuilding and infrastructure will be needed to support new communications and technology wages are also likely to increase.

According to the September 2021 Bureau of Labor Statistics,[1]

OCCUPATION	JOB SUMMARY	Entry-Level Education	2020 MEDIAN PAY
Aerospace Engineering & Operations Technologists & Technicians	Aerospace engineering and operations technologists and technicians run and maintain equipment used to develop, test, produce, and sustain aircraft and spacecraft.	Associate's Degree	$68,570
Aerospace Engineers	Aerospace engineers design primarily aircraft, spacecraft, satellites, and missiles.	Bachelor's Degree	$118,610
Agricultural Engineers	Agricultural engineers solve problems concerning power supplies, machine efficiency, the use of structures and facilities, pollution and environmental issues, and the storage and processing of agricultural products.	Bachelor's Degree	$84,410
Architects	Architects plan and design houses, factories, office buildings, and other structures.	Bachelor's Degree	$82,320
Bioengineers & Biomedical Engineers	Bioengineers and biomedical engineers combine engineering principles with sciences to design and create equipment, devices, computer systems, and software.	Bachelor's Degree	$92,620
Cartographers & Photogrammetrists	Cartographers and photogrammetrists collect, measure, and interpret geographic information in order to create and update maps and charts for regional planning, education, and other purposes.	Bachelor's Degree	$68,380
Chemical Engineers	Chemical engineers apply the principles of chemistry, biology, physics, and math to solve problems that involve the use of fuel, drugs, food, and many other products.	Bachelor's Degree	$108,540
Civil Engineering Technologists & Technicians	Civil engineering technologists and technicians help civil engineers plan, design, and build infrastructure and development projects.	Associate's Degree	$54,080

---

1   Occupational Outlook Handbook, "Architecture and Engineering Occupations," *U.S. Bureau of Labor Statistics*, September 8, 2021, https://www.bls.gov/ooh/architecture-and-engineering/home.htm

OCCUPATION	JOB SUMMARY	Entry-Level Education	2020 MEDIAN PAY
Civil Engineers	Civil engineers design, build, and supervise infrastructure projects and systems.	Bachelor's Degree	$88,570
Computer Hardware Engineers	Computer hardware engineers research, design, develop, and test computer systems and components.	Bachelor's Degree	$119,560
Drafters	Drafters use software to convert the designs of engineers and architects into technical drawings.	Associate's Degree	$57,960
Electrical & Electronic Engineering Technologists & Technicians	Electrical and electronic engineering technologists and technicians help engineers design and develop equipment that is powered by electricity or electric current.	Associate's Degree	$67,550
Electrical & Electronics Engineers	Electrical engineers design, develop, test, and supervise the manufacture of electrical equipment.	Bachelor's Degree	$103,390
Electro-mechanical & Mechatronics Technologists & Technicians	Electro-mechanical and mechatronics technologists and technicians operate, test, and maintain electromechanical or robotic equipment.	Associate's Degree	$59,800
Environmental Engineering Technologists & Technicians	Environmental engineering technologists and technicians implement the plans that environmental engineers develop.	Associate's Degree	$51,630
Environmental Engineers	Environmental engineers use the principles of engineering, soil science, biology, and chemistry to develop solutions to environmental problems.	Bachelor's Degree	$92,120
Health & Safety Engineers	Health and safety engineers combine knowledge of engineering and of health and safety to develop procedures and design systems to protect people from illness and injury and property from damage.	Bachelor's Degree	$94,240
Industrial Engineering Technologists & Technicians	Industrial engineering technologists and technicians help engineers solve problems affecting manufacturing layout or production.	Associate's Degree	$57,320
Industrial Engineers	Industrial engineers devise efficient systems that integrate workers, machines, materials, information, and energy to make a product or provide a service.	Bachelor's Degree	$88,950
Landscape Architects	Landscape architects design parks and other outdoor spaces.	Bachelor's Degree	$70,630
Marine Engineers & Naval Architects	Marine engineers and naval architects design, build, and maintain ships, from aircraft carriers to submarines and from sailboats to tankers.	Bachelor's Degree	$95,440

OCCUPATION	JOB SUMMARY	Entry-Level Education	2020 MEDIAN PAY
Materials Engineers	Materials engineers develop, process, and test materials used to create a wide range of products.	Bachelor's Degree	$95,640
Mechanical Engineering Technologists & Technicians	Mechanical engineering technologists and technicians help mechanical engineers design, develop, test, and manufacture machines and other devices.	Associate's Degree	$58,230
Mechanical Engineers	Mechanical engineers design, develop, build, and test mechanical and thermal sensors and devices.	Bachelor's Degree	$90,160
Mining & Geological Engineers	Mining and geological engineers design mines to safely and efficiently remove minerals for use in manufacturing and utilities.	Bachelor's Degree	$93,800
Nuclear Engineers	Nuclear engineers research and develop the processes, instruments, and systems used to derive benefits from nuclear energy and radiation.	Bachelor's Degree	$116,140
Petroleum Engineers	Petroleum engineers design and develop methods for extracting oil and gas from deposits below the Earth's surface.	Bachelor's Degree	$137,330
Surveying & Mapping Technicians	Surveying and mapping technicians collect data and make maps of the Earth's surface.	High School Diploma or Equivalent	$46,200
Surveyors	Surveyors make precise measurements to determine property boundaries.	Bachelor's Degree	$65,590

We know what we are but know not what we may be.

– William Shakespeare

While architects work in studios where they design plans for living areas where people work, shop, study, worship, and enjoy their free time, some of their time is spent in consultation with planners, engineers, and other architects. The work of an architect is a cross between artist, inventor, and engineer. The median pay for an architect is $82,320 for those with a B.Arch. Those with an M.Arch. are typically paid higher. The employment prospects for architects are positive, but slower than average compared to other occupations.

Similar jobs are listed in the previous chart, but typically include engineers, designers, drafters, surveyors, and urban and regional planners. The skills an architecture student learns in school, including computer-aided design and

drafting (CADD) and other software, are also valuable in other fields. According to the Bureau of Labor Statistics, approximately 17% of architects are self-employed while 3% work in government, 3% in construction, and the remaining 71% work for engineering or architecture companies.[2]

According to 2021 National Council of Architectural Registration Boards (NCARB) data, approximately 40% of architects are women and over half of all architects identify as people of color. In the last ten years, gender representation improved 10% and ethnic diversity improved 16%.[3] Women complete licensure requirements one year sooner than men. Canada has the largest number of NCARB licensures, outnumbering the U.S., U.K., China, and the Republic of Korea combined.

IMPACT OF COVID-19

COVID-19 impacted the number of licensure completions. For the ARE exam, there was a 44% drop in the number of people taking the test and a 42% drop in the number of successful completions.[4] In raw numbers, 29,394 exams were taken while only 2,702 successfully completed the test. Given the impact of the virus and economy, there was a 20% drop in work experience reported through the AXP. In all, 33% fewer candidates started the path to licensure in 2020 and there were 40% fewer new architects.

2   Occupational Outlook Handbook, "Architects: Work Environment," *U.S. Bureau of Labor Statistics,* September 8, 2021, https://www.bls.gov/ooh/architecture-and-engineering/architects.htm#tab-3

3   NCARB, "Demographics: Career and Licensure," *NCARB*, 2021, https://www.ncarb.org/nbtn2021/demographics-licensure

4   NCARB, "COVID-19's Impact on Licensure," *NCARB*, 2021, https://www.ncarb.org/nbtn2021/covid19

The impact of COVID-19 cannot be understated. However, there are now 121,997 architects in the United States' 55 jurisdictions, representing a 5% increase. At this moment, there are 30,453 candidates actively pursuing licensure. Though only 2,863 completed the requirements, representing a 29% drop.[5]

ROAD TO LICENSURE

The road to licensure is long. The average time to complete licensure is 12.3 years, though Asian candidates take less time on average. This should not be discouraging. There are quite a few steps to take along the way. Even so, achieving the goal is rewarding. Encourage those around you. If this is the field you want to pursue, pave the road in front of you and drive. An internship or apprenticeship or two would not hurt you in your pursuit of a position at a good firm. Although some internships are unpaid, you will find that most applicants will have one or more. Some internships pay fairly well.

If you are serious, you will make a fantastic career out of your pursuit. Initiative-taking persistence, talent, creativity, and moxie can get you into your desired college program and career. You may have to start at the very bottom of the ladder, but you can climb the rungs methodically one by one.

Companies want to know the work ethic, personality, and professionalism of any employees they choose. An internship allows you to get to know their corporate climate better and allows them to get to know you better too. Thus, many companies hire the interns they feel are the best fit rather than choosing candidates from the piles of resumes that have been submitted.

Education unlocks doors no matter which direction your career takes you. Whatever avenue you pursue, if you lay a foundation, undaunted by the competition, and are unafraid of starting at the bottom, you will do fine. Hard work and creativity go a long way in this industry. Start by getting a solid education.

MANAGEMENT AND EMPLOYEE RETENTION

Skills to Know: Management, Human Resources, Social Consciousness, Ethics

One of the most significant challenges facing employers in the years from 2022 - 2030 will be locating and retaining talent. The pandemic slowed education

---

5   NCARB, "Demographics: AXP and ARE," *NCARB*, 2021, https://www.ncarb.org/nbtn2021/demographics-axp-are

and learning with online classes, reduced access to faculty/advising, limited access to labs, inability to attend workshops, retail closures, and fewer conferences, meetings, and shows. Health concerns rose to the top of importance as did financial stress, job uncertainty, and social consciousness.

Many students chose to work rather than study and start online stores when they could not access locations for community service or continue with their sport, instrument, or hobbies. With the changes in lifestyle and fears about health, safety, and wellness, many bright and talented students developed a fearless sense of autonomy and independence, while for others, the necessary skills ordinarily developed in school were fraught by limitations.

Finding talent within the changing hiring atmosphere will require new skills to retain staff. Employees are increasingly looking elsewhere for a better opportunity. This development will require managers to earn and harness employee trust and loyalty.

The digital workforce has also placed demands on human resources. While many companies want their employees to work in-person, the convenience of working at home and the drudgery of commuting to work have created an environment where employees seek greater flexibility. Changes are coming. The employee talent challenge is likely to create a more global workforce where companies look for less expensive online talent from a pool of eager workers in other countries.

CHAPTER 10

NEXT STEPS: PREPARATION AND REAL-WORLD SKILLS

"Buildings are deeply emotive structures which form our psyche."

– David Adjaye

Experience the dynamic, multidimensional world of architecture. In some careers, repetitive tasks and uninspiring projects lead employees to loathe their jobs and tick off minutes until their day is done. Meanwhile, architecture is about creating, inventing, and energizing. With a minimum of 3,740 supervised field hours required for licensure through the Architectural Experience Program (AXP), architects earn their way to a career of endless possibilities.

American philosopher, Criss Jami, shared, "Find a purpose to serve, not a lifestyle to live." Thus, as architects contemplate their work, one consideration is how to enhance our world by designing intriguing, fulfilling, uplifting, and environmentally sustainable solutions to our world's towns and cities. The interior spaces in Singapore's ParkRoyal Hotel are as captivating as its exterior. Throughout history, societal purpose and functional necessities changed; service never goes out of style.

The B.Arch. or M.Arch. along with requisite licensure is a necessary beginning. Attending a respected school can help you get noticed. Your next steps are aided by connections through professors, classmates, and alumni. Networking at events is also an excellent way to discover opportunities. Shows, displays, and contests in school, out of school, in the summer, or through social media can help you get noticed.

Throughout your varied experiences, you will meet other architects who can recommend you or let you know about open positions or contract opportunities, even some that are not publicly announced. Many schools have a culminating showcase where you can put your best foot forward. Exposure to industry professionals helps. Interacting with people online or in-person also allows you to maintain those connections.

Autonomy and freedom to choose the jobs you take by starting your own architecture firm may seem alluring but there are numerous drawbacks. Some of these challenges may result in uncertainty or even career limitations. Firms often choose seasoned professionals. However, there are ways to mitigate against the lean times of solo work. Demonstrating mastery, resolving client problems, aligning ideologies, and charging less are a few options. Even so, you need to put yourself out there.

You could wait for the phone to ring to be discovered. However, you should be out and about for that to happen. Some individuals pine away, hoping to be selected and deciding which organization would be a perfect fit. Others decide that they only want to work at a specific firm or location. Still others determine that they will work for themselves and be their own boss. Yet, sometimes taking any type of position at the start is a steppingstone to the dream life, commitment to service, or opportunity to put your unique mark on society.

BOLD NETWORKING

Networking takes social skills and a bit of moxie. From elevator speeches and professional encounters to interviews and masterclasses, your job is to find a way to get in front of people and have them see your work and your potential to contribute. You have something special and fresh ideas. There is a professional entity that will welcome your style, ingenuity, discipline, and impact.

How can you be recognized? Meet people; hand out your resume; give them your business card; ask for their business card; follow up; ask if you can call or meet them, even when approaching these professionals may seem uncomfortable. Stay in touch with people you meet, even if it is just happenstance or serendipity. Keep a log with each person's phone, e-mail, identifying information, and both date and location where you met. You never know when you will need it.

If you meet people professionally at a masterclass or workshop, even if you do not exchange information, you will recognize them at a later date. They may recognize you in a future event too. Keep training. You should always want to improve and seek ways to improve irrespective of your experience. The outside world's perspective changes more quickly with social media's instant influences. Imagine how towns, cities, and landscapes should look and ways they could be more livable also.

Though you should not take workshops just for the sake of meeting people, be present in your quest to lead, serve, and envision. If your focus is not on your improvement or development, you may appear insincere in your intentions. However, workshops, conferences, and contests can allow others to see your purpose, vision, and talent.

Big-ticket training events do not always mean better trainers or opportunities. Find time to go to museums, survey your surroundings, and notice cultural changes. While you are gathering new thoughts, remember that humility and open-mindedness go a long way. Defer to the wise and listen. There is much you can learn. Buckminster Fuller stated, "Dare to be naïve."

STAY IN TOUCH

Do not annoy busy people, but you can keep in touch every couple of months. Communicating more frequently is overwhelming. However, life is long. People who grow with their craft, transition fluidly through life's career phases. In architecture, contacts are important in all phases of your career. Also, do not be surprised. Many go-getters, seeking to gain a coveted contract do the following:

1.   Speak at Chamber of Commerce meetings
2.   Attend building, construction, and industry trade shows
3.   Gain a following on Instagram and Pinterest
4.   Write a newsletter and publish it on LinkedIn and other sources
5.   Link your work to Facebook, Twitter, and other social media.
6.   Enter in design contests
7.   Join professional associations
8.   Attend social gatherings of potential customers
9.   Keep in touch with your professors
10. Stay involved with your alumni associations

Friendships matter. Become lifelong colleagues, by finding friends who share mutual interests and offer a sounding board or connections to new opportunities. People tend to stay in touch with "important" people. Note to self: Your contemporaries or peers are important people...although possibly not yet. As you form lists of contacts, you are likely to know these people throughout your career.

Be audacious, while also being authentic. Networking can sometimes appear fake or forced, as if you are going out on a hunt to find people for your own benefit. Worse, the act of networking can appear like stalking for those who incessantly attempt to connect.

The mental image of this type of 'networking' conjures the vision of people congregating at meetings. Friendships and the mutual support of allies can be enormously helpful, though 20,000 or even 200,000 followers on your website do not mean you are popular or important. However, you can have unexpected meaningful exchanges if you get out, meet people, and live life.

There are times when deeply moving, casual conversations in non-professional settings could also turn into connections. Do not lose touch with people or burn bridges along the way. This industry is not that big, and you will continually see movers and shakers on all levels. You never know. They may contact you to collaborate one day or meet for coffee at an event.

COLLEGE AND CAREER CENTERS

Although architecture programs often have internal connections to help you secure an internship or job, you might also speak to someone at your campus career center. They often have interesting and possibly different prospects you might not get elsewhere. There may be a specific career liaison for architecture. Connect with them for help in your search process. Besides, you might just want to get a related job that utilizes your creative, design, problem-solving, and presentation skills.

Companies that attend building, construction, and engineering trade shows often hire new architecture majors. Their energy, initiative, and cutting-edge knowledge are invaluable. Marketing companies also appreciate those who can explain the utility of their products. These jobs may not be your ideal, but sometimes you just need a position to earn money and get yourself on your feet.

Career center coordinators often have excellent ideas of alternative options you may have never considered. Furthermore, they can assist you with creating a professional resume and cover letters for specific industries that are different from the ones you have for architecture.

They may also connect you with past graduates in the industry who make excellent connections. Some of them may have been in your program and have been through the ropes, know a few people, and may be able to get you an interview or invite you to an industry event. Any contact may be able to get your foot into the door or a job to make money in the meantime.

LINKEDIN

LinkedIn is especially helpful for career searches. You can find numerous influential contacts on LinkedIn. After interviews or events, connect with each person you met on LinkedIn. Keep a contact list of individuals you know in the architecture world. Do not constantly try to connect with people you do not really know. However, if you have made the connection, occasionally keep in touch.

While some LinkedIn message boxes may be full and you may not get a reply, you can try. Some people have tens of thousands of LinkedIn followers. I have about 20,000, which does not make me important. Remember that a paycheck or lots of friends does not make you more worthy or successful. Worth and value emanate from within your heart. Occasionally, you hit on a lucky break. Though I do not have time to communicate with everyone, I have connected with some of my most inspiring authors, advisors, and intellectual leaders through LinkedIn.

FINALLY

Most people are willing to help you. Five percent will not. Thus, you have a 19 out of 20 chance of interacting with decent people who have the time and will give you advice. Don't lose faith in humanity just because you run into a few people who are too busy to stop for you or are too self-absorbed that they cannot answer your question.

Remember that talent is only the beginning you need to sell yourself. As you organize your goals and responsibilities remember to think one step ahead of where you want to be by making a game plan. Since actions speak louder than words, take action without complaining and spread kindness along the way. Burned bridges are very hard to reconstruct.

Honesty and trustworthiness are worth more than any physical object. Earn this by working hard, being efficient, and telling the truth. Acting professionally in your words and deeds is essential. Put away all distractions and focus on your tasks. Texts and social media take a surprising amount of time. Every action you take is a steppingstone to your future. Discipline is achieved by creating a goal and making it happen.

A nice note, card, or gift reminds people you are thinking about them when you are really busy. Good friends who have your best interest may know doors that are not yet open for you. Keep in touch with them.

So, go on a walk; meet people; and live fully. Serendipity happens when you live life. However, your education is immensely valuable. Success happens when preparation meets opportunity. Thus, preparation is the best way to generate luck. Finally, even the most disciplined person can be lazy or inefficient. Fight this. Stay active. Make your life happen for you. Here are a few things to remember as you go out to pursue your dreams.

- Work ethic is everything.
- Excellence is expected.
- Learn what you do not know on your own time.
- Come to work prepared.
- Take constructive criticism well.
- Be respectful and courteous.
- Keep your cool under pressure.
- Avoid being timid.
- Stay on task.
- Come early.
- Stay late.
- Take your work seriously.
- Do more than expected.
- Be thoughtful and respectful.
- Read your e-mail/texts after hours in case something is important.
- Ask questions. No question is too stupid.
- Maintain a clean workspace.
- Dress and act professionally.
- Don't gossip or complain.
- Play when you are done.
- Avoid frustrating your phenomenally busy supervisor.
- Be straightforward, and don't beat around the bush.

You've Got This!

4
Regions

60
Programs

COLLEGE
PROFILES AND
REQUIREMENTS

WEST

MIDWEST

NORTHEAST

SOUTH

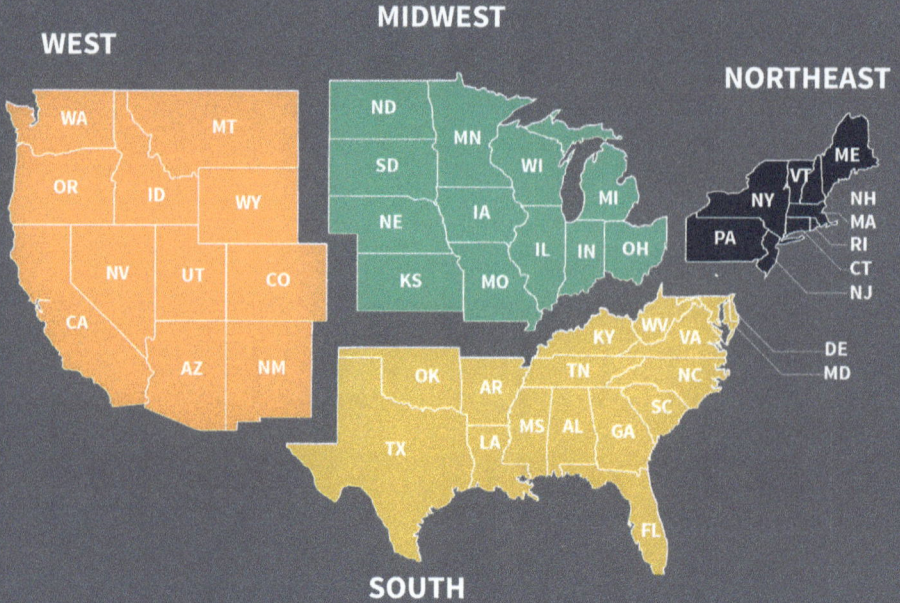

PROGRAMS BY REGION
U.S. CENSUS BUREAU CLASSIFICATIONS

REGION 1 – NORTHEAST

Connecticut, Maine, Massachusetts, New Hampshire, New Jersey, New York, Pennsylvania, Rhode Island, and Vermont

REGION 2 – MIDWEST

Illinois, Indiana, Iowa, Kansas, Michigan, Minnesota, Missouri, Nebraska, North Dakota, Ohio, South Dakota, and Wisconsin

REGION 3 – SOUTH

Alabama, Arkansas, Delaware, District of Columbia, Florida, Georgia, Kentucky, Louisiana, Maryland, Mississippi, North Carolina, Oklahoma, South Carolina, Tennessee, Texas, Virginia, and West Virginia

REGION 4 – WEST

Alaska, Arizona, California, Colorado, Hawaii, Idaho, Montana, Nevada, New Mexico, Oregon, Utah, Washington, and Wyoming

LIST OF ARCHITECTURE PROGRAMS

The 60 programs listed in the following pages include the top 25-ranked architecture programs along with a number of additional schools with undergraduate architecture programs that offer various degrees – some licensure-directed and some with B.A. or B.S. programs. Many students interested in architecture are also interested in city planning, building science, or urban design. An effort was made to add these programs when available as of March 2022.

Architecture programs with B.Arch. or M.Arch. have studio requirements and the coursework is often difficult. Students often look for similar career paths since the road to architecture licensure is arduous and long. Architecture is not for everyone. Although immensely rewarding, there are challenges. Students discover what is most important to them along the way and may choose an alternative path somewhere down the road.

Thus, this book aims to provide you with a more comprehensive set of lists so that you can explore your options. Keep the book handy. Even after you begin college, you may find the additional programs in the back are helpful for connections or summer programs.

Creating lists is often tedious and cumbersome. These lists were gathered to help you with this task.

Descriptions of the college programs, tuition, requirements, and deadlines are accurate as of March 2022. The requirements may have changed somewhat by the time you purchase this book, but this information is a great place to start!

Note: To simplify the text and fit information into the charts and descriptions, abbreviations were used as well as shortened sentences and acronyms.

CONNECTICUT

MAINE

MASSACHUSETTS

NEW HAMPSHIRE

NEW JERSEY

NEW YORK

PENNSYLVANIA

RHODE ISLAND

VERMONT

CHAPTER 11

REGION ONE

NORTHEAST

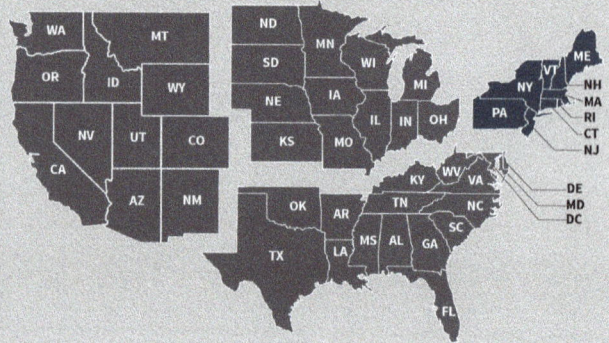

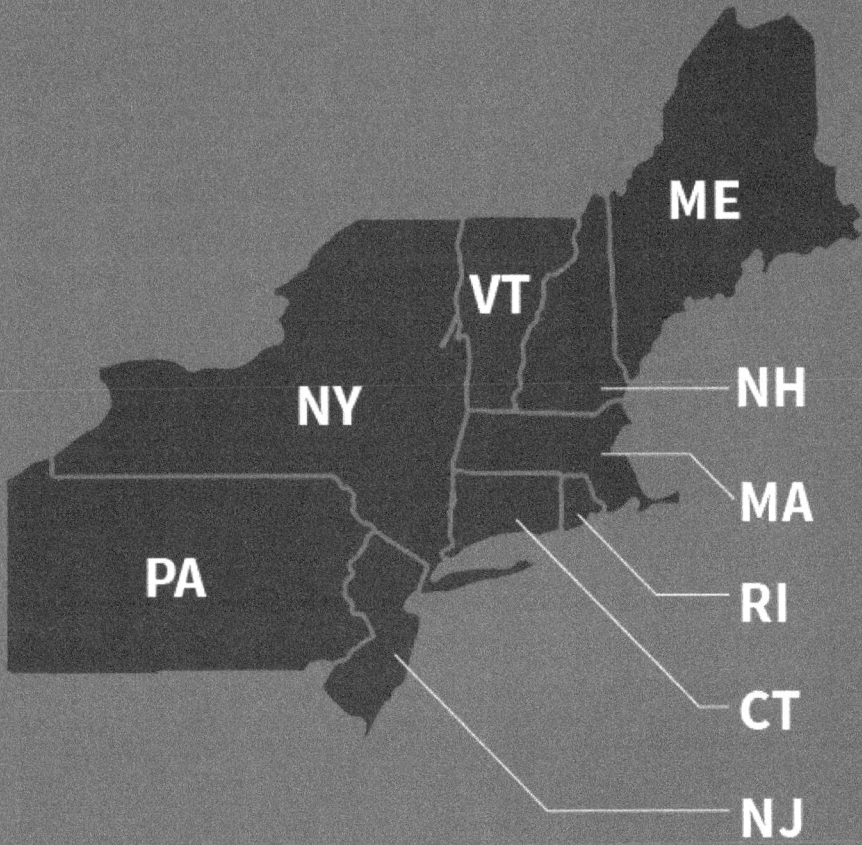

20 *Programs* | **9** *States*

1. CT - Yale University
2. MA - Boston Architectural College
3. MA - Harvard University
4. MA - Massachusetts Institute of Technology (MIT)
5. MA - Northeastern University
6. NJ - New Jersey Institute of Technology (NJIT)
7. NJ - Princeton University
8. NY - The City College of New York - CUNY
9. NY - The Cooper Union
10. NY - Cornell University
11. NY - New York Institute of Technology (NYIT)
12. NY - Pratt Institute
13. NY - Rensselaer Polytechnic Institute (RPI)
14. NY - SUNY College of Technology at Alfred State University
15. NY - Syracuse University
16. PA - Carnegie Mellon University
17. PA - Pennsylvania State University (Penn State)
18. PA - Thomas Jefferson University
19. PA - University of Pennsylvania (UPenn)
20. RI - Rhode Island School of Design (RISD)

ARCHITECTURE PROGRAMS

School	Avg. GPA, SAT Evidence-Based Reading Writing (ERW), SAT Math (M), and ACT Composite (C) Early Decision (ED): Yes/No	Admission Statistics	Program(s)	Portfolio Required (req.)
Yale University 220 York Street, room 102, New Haven, CT 06511	GPA: N/A SAT (ERW): 720-780 SAT (M): 740-800 ACT (C): 33-35 ED: No, but Restrictive Early Action (REA) available	Overall College Admit Rate: 7% Undergrad Enrollment: 4,664 Total Enrollment: 12,060	B.A. Architecture Degrees Awarded in the Program(s): 22	Portfolio not req.

School	Avg. GPA, SAT Evidence-Based Reading Writing (ERW), SAT Math (M), and ACT Composite (C) Early Decision (ED): Yes/No	Admission Statistics	Program(s)	Portfolio Required (req.)
Boston Architectural College 320 Newbury St., Boston, MA 02115	GPA: N/A* SAT (ERW): N/A* SAT (M): N/A* ACT (C): N/A* *Open admissions ED: No	Overall College Admit Rate: N/A* Undergrad Enrollment: 336 Total Enrollment: 742 *Open admissions	Bachelor of Architecture (B.Arch.) - 5-year B.S. Architecture Bachelor of Interior Architecture Bachelor of Landscape Architecture (B.L.A.) Graduate Degree(s): Master of Architecture (M.Arch.) Master of Interior Architecture Master of Landscape Architecture (M.L.A.) Master of Design Studies in Design for Human Health Master of Design Studies in Historic Preservation Degrees Awarded in the Program(s): N/A	Portfolio optional

NORTHEAST

School	Avg. GPA, SAT Evidence-Based Reading Writing (ERW), SAT Math (M), and ACT Composite (C) Early Decision (ED): Yes/No	Admission Statistics	Program(s)	Portfolio Required (req.)
Harvard University Harvard University, Massachusetts Hall, Cambridge, MA 02138	GPA: 4.22 SAT (ERW): 720-780 SAT (M): 740-800 ACT (C): 33-35 ED: Yes	Overall College Admit Rate: 5% Undergrad Enrollment: 8,527 Total Enrollment: 30,391	A.B in History of Art and Architecture Graduate Degree(s): M.Arch., MLA, Master in Urban Planning, Master in Design Engineering Ph.D. Architecture, Landscape Architecture and Urban Planning Doctor of Design Degrees Awarded in the Program(s): N/A	Portfolio optional
Massachusetts Institute of Technology (MIT) 77 Massachusetts Ave, Cambridge, MA 02139	GPA: N/A SAT (ERW): 730-780 SAT (M): 780-800 ACT (C): 34-36 ED: No	Overall College Admit Rate: 7% Undergrad Enrollment: 4,361 Total Enrollment: 11,254	B.S. Architecture B.S. Art & Design Graduate degrees: Master of Architecture (M.Arch.) Degrees Awarded in the Program(s): 12	Portfolio optional

School	Avg. GPA, SAT Evidence-Based Reading Writing (ERW), SAT Math (M), and ACT Composite (C) Early Decision (ED): Yes/No	Admission Statistics	Program(s)	Portfolio Required (req.)
Northeastern University 360 Huntington Ave, Boston, MA 02115	GPA: N/A SAT (ERW): 690-750 SAT (M): 720-790 ACT (C): 34-36 ED: Yes	Overall College Admit Rate: 20% Undergrad Enrollment: 15,156 Total Enrollment: 22,905	B.S. Architecture Graduate Degree(s): Master of Architecture (M.Arch.) Degrees Awarded in the Program(s): 46	Portfolio optional

NORTHEAST

ARCHITECTURE PROGRAMS

School	Avg. GPA, SAT Evidence-Based Reading Writing (ERW), SAT Math (M), and ACT Composite (C) Early Decision (ED): Yes/No	Admission Statistics	Program(s)	Portfolio Required (req.)
New Jersey Institute of Technology (NJIT) Weston Hall 340, University Heights, Newark, NJ 07102	GPA: 3.59 SAT (ERW): 590-670 SAT (M): 610-720 ACT (C): 25-31 ED: No	Overall College Admit Rate: 66% Undergrad Enrollment: 9,084 Total Enrollment: 11,652	Bachelor of Architecture (B.Arch.) - 5-year B.S. Architecture Graduate Degree(s): Master of Architecture (M.Arch.) M.S. Architecture Master of Urban Design M.Arch. and Infrastructure Planning (M.I.P.) M.Arch. and Civil Engineering (M.S.) M.Arch. and Master of Business Administration (M.B.A.) Ph.D. Urban Systems Degrees Awarded in the Program(s): 56	Portfolio req.

School	Avg. GPA, SAT Evidence-Based Reading Writing (ERW), SAT Math (M), and ACT Composite (C) Early Decision (ED): Yes/No	Admission Statistics	Program(s)	Portfolio Required (req.)
Princeton University Princeton University, Princeton, NJ 08544	GPA: 3.93 SAT (ERW): 710-770 SAT (M): 740-800 ACT (C): 32-35 ED: No, but Restrictive Early Action (REA) available	Overall College Admit Rate: 6% Undergrad Enrollment: 4,774 Total Enrollment: 7,853	A.B. with a concentration in Architecture Degrees Awarded in the Program(s): 16	Portfolio req.
The City College of New York - CUNY 141 Convent Avenue, New York, NY 10031	GPA: 3.34 SAT (ERW): 650-750 SAT (M): 655-790 ACT (C): 30-35 ED: No	Overall College Admit Rate: 51% Undergrad Enrollment: 12,587 Total Enrollment: 15,227	Bachelor of Architecture (B.Arch.) - 5-year B.S. Architectural Studies Graduate Degree(s): Master of Architecture (M.Arch.) M.S. Architecture Master of Landscape Architecture (M.L.A.) Master of Urban Planning Master of Urban Sustainability Degrees Awarded in the Program(s): 49	Portfolio req.

NORTHEAST

ARCHITECTURE PROGRAMS

School	Avg. GPA, SAT Evidence-Based Reading Writing (ERW), SAT Math (M), and ACT Composite (C) / Early Decision (ED): Yes/No	Admission Statistics	Program(s)	Portfolio Required (req.)
The Cooper Union 30 Cooper Sq, New York, NY 10003	GPA: 3.75 SAT (ERW): 650-740 SAT (M): 655-790 ACT (C): 30-35 ED: Yes	Overall College Admit Rate: 18% Undergrad Enrollment: 806 Total Enrollment: 887	Bachelor of Architecture (B.Arch.) - 5-year Graduate Degree(s): M.S. Architecture Degrees Awarded in the Program(s): 15	Portfolio req.
Cornell University 139 Sibley Dome, Cornell University, Ithaca, NY 14853	GPA: N/A SAT (ERW): 680-750 SAT (M): 720-790 ACT (C): 32-35 ED: Yes	Overall College Admit Rate: 11% Undergrad Enrollment: 14,743 Total Enrollment: 23,620	Bachelor of Architecture (B.Arch.) - 5-year Degrees Awarded in the Program(s): 125	Portfolio req.

School	Avg. GPA, SAT Evidence-Based Reading Writing (ERW), SAT Math (M), and ACT Composite (C) Early Decision (ED): Yes/No	Admission Statistics	Program(s)	Portfolio Required (req.)
New York Institute of Technology (NYIT) 1855 Broadway, New York, NY 10023	GPA: 3.4 SAT (ERW): 520-630 SAT (M): 540-660 ACT (C): 23-30 ED: No	Overall College Admit Rate: 75% Undergrad Enrollment: 3,473 Total Enrollment: 6,851	Bachelor of Architecture (B.Arch.) - 5-year B.S. Architectural Technology, concentrations: Construction Management Graduate Degree(s): Master of Architecture (M.Arch.) M.S. Architecture, Health and Design M.S. Architecture, Computational Technologies M.S. Architecture, Urban Design Degrees Awarded in the Program(s): 93	Portfolio req.

NORTHEAST

ARCHITECTURE PROGRAMS

School	Avg. GPA, SAT Evidence-Based Reading Writing (ERW), SAT Math (M), and ACT Composite (C) Early Decision (ED): Yes/No	Admission Statistics	Program(s)	Portfolio Required (req.)
Pratt Institute 200 Willoughby Avenue, Brooklyn, NY 11205	GPA: 3.82 SAT (ERW): 570-660 SAT (M): 550-680 ACT (C): 25-30 ED: No	Overall College Admit Rate: 66% Undergrad Enrollment: 3,122 Total Enrollment: 4,353	Bachelor of Architecture (B.Arch.) - 5-year B.S. Construction Management Graduate Degree(s) Master of Architecture (M.Arch.) M.S. Architecture Degrees Awarded in the Program(s): 132	Portfolio req.
Rensselaer Polytechnic Institute (RPI) 110 8th Street, Greene Bldg., Troy, NY 12180	GPA: 3.91 SAT (ERW): 620-720 SAT (M): 680-780 ACT (C): 29-34 ED: Yes	Overall College Admit Rate: 57% Undergrad Enrollment: 6,283 Total Enrollment: 7,501	Bachelor of Architecture (B.Arch.) - 5-year B.S. Building Sciences Degrees Awarded in the Program(s): 44	Portfolio req.
SUNY College of Technology at Alfred State University 10 Upper College Dr., Alfred, NY 14802	GPA: N/A SAT (ERW): 470-580 SAT (M): 470-590 ACT (C): 18-25 ED: No	Overall College Admit Rate: 72% Undergrad Enrollment: 257 Total Enrollment: 3,667	Bachelor of Architecture (B.Arch.) - 5-year B.S. Architectural Technology Degrees Awarded in the Program(s): 14	B.Arch. Portfolio req. B.S. Portfolio not req.

School	Avg. GPA, SAT Evidence-Based Reading Writing (ERW), SAT Math (M), and ACT Composite (C) Early Decision (ED): Yes/No	Admission Statistics	Program(s)	Portfolio Required (req.)
Syracuse University 201 Slocum Hall, Syracuse, NY 13244	GPA: 3.67 SAT (ERW): N/A SAT (M): N/A ACT (C): N/A ED: Yes	Overall College Admit Rate: 69% Undergrad Enrollment: 14,479 Total Enrollment: 21,322	Bachelor of Architecture (B.Arch.) - 5-year Degrees Awarded in the Program(s): 117	Portfolio req.
Carnegie Mellon University 5000 Forbes Avenue, Pittsburgh, PA 15213	GPA: 3.85 SAT (ERW): 700-760 SAT (M): 760-800 ACT (C): 33-35 ED: Yes	Overall College Admit Rate: 17% Undergrad Enrollment: 7,073 Total Enrollment: 14,189	Bachelor of Architecture (B.Arch.) - 5-year B.A. Architecture BXA Intercollege Degree Degrees Awarded in the Program(s): 48	Portfolio req.

NORTHEAST

ARCHITECTURE PROGRAMS

School	Avg. GPA, SAT Evidence-Based Reading Writing (ERW), SAT Math (M), and ACT Composite (C) Early Decision (ED): Yes/No	Admission Statistics	Program(s)	Portfolio Required (req.)
Pennsylvania State University (Penn State) 124 Borland Building, University Park, PA 16802	GPA: N/A SAT (ERW): 580-670 SAT (M): 580-700 ACT (C): 25-30 ED: No	Overall College Admit Rate: 49% Undergrad Enrollment: 40,639 Total Enrollment: 47,223	Bachelor of Architecture (B.Arch.) - 5-year Graduate Degree(s) Master of Architecture (M.Arch.) M.S. Architecture Dual M.S. Architecture and HDNRE Ph.D. Architecture Dual Ph.D. Architecture and HDNRE Degrees Awarded in the Program(s): 62	Portfolio not req.

School	Avg. GPA, SAT Evidence-Based Reading Writing (ERW), SAT Math (M), and ACT Composite (C) Early Decision (ED): Yes/No	Admission Statistics	Program(s)	Portfolio Required (req.)
Thomas Jefferson University 4201 Henry Avenue, Philadelphia, PA 19144	GPA: N/A SAT (ERW): 550-630 SAT (M): 540-640 ACT (C): 20-27 ED: No	Overall College Admit Rate: 70% Undergrad Enrollment: 3,783 Total Enrollment: 8,286	Bachelor of Architecture (B.Arch.) - 5-year B.S. Architectural Studies B.S. Construction Management B.S. Interior Design Bachelor of Landscape Architecture (B.L.A.) Graduate Degree(s) Master of Architecture (M.Arch.) M.S. Architecture M.S. Construction Management M.S. Geospatial Technology for Geodesign M.S. Historic PReservation M.S. Interior Architecture M.S. Real Estate Development M.S. Sustainable Design Master of Urban Design (M.U.D.) Degrees Awarded in the Program(s): 70	Portfolio optional

NORTHEAST

ARCHITECTURE PROGRAMS

School	Avg. GPA, SAT Evidence-Based Reading Writing (ERW), SAT Math (M), and ACT Composite (C) Early Decision (ED): Yes/No	Admission Statistics	Program(s)	Portfolio Required (req.)
University of Pennsylvania (UPenn) University of Pennsylvania, Philadelphia, PA 19104	GPA: 3.9 SAT (ERW): 710-770 SAT (M): 750-800 ACT (C): 33-35 ED: Yes	Overall College Admit Rate: 9% Undergrad Enrollment: 11,155 Total Enrollment: 26,552	B.A. Architecture Graduate Degree(s) Master of Architecture (M.Arch.) Master of City Planning Master of Landscape Architecture (M.L.A.) Master of Environmental Building Design Master of Urban Spatial Analytics M.S. Architecture M.S. Design: Advanced Architectural Design (M.S.D-A.A.D.) M.S. Design: Environmental Building Design (M.S.D.-E.B.D.) M.S. Design: Historic Preservation M.S. Design: Robotics and Autonomous Systems (M.S.D.-R.A.S.) M.S. Historic Preservation Ph.D. Architecture Ph.D. City and Regional Planning Degrees Awarded in the Program(s): 15	Portfolio not req.

School	Avg. GPA, SAT Evidence-Based Reading Writing (ERW), SAT Math (M), and ACT Composite (C) Early Decision (ED): Yes/No	Admission Statistics	Program(s)	Portfolio Required (req.)
Rhode Island School of Design (RISD) 2 College St, Providence, RI 02903	GPA: N/A SAT (ERW): 610-700 SAT (M): 640-770 ACT (C): 27-32 ED: Yes	Overall College Admit Rate: 27% Undergrad Enrollment: 1,736 Total Enrollment: 2,227	Bachelor of Architecture (B.Arch.) - 5-year Degrees Awarded in the Program(s): 77	Portfolio req.

NORTHEAST

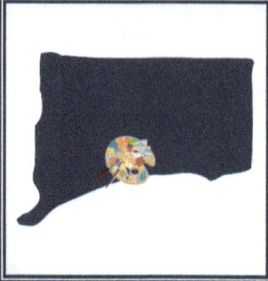

CONNECTICUT

MAINE

MASSACHUSETTS

NEW HAMPSHIRE

NEW JERSEY

NEW YORK

PENNSYLVANIA

RHODE ISLAND

VERMONT

YALE UNIVERSITY

Address: 220 York Street, room 102, New Haven, CT 06511
Website: *https://www.architecture.yale.edu/academics/undergraduate-studies*
Contact: *https://www.yale.edu/contact-us*
Phone: (203) 432-4771
Email: student.questions@yale.edu

COST OF ATTENDANCE:

Tuition & Fees: $59,950 | **Additional Expenses:** $21,625
Total: $81,575

Financial Aid: https://www.yale.edu/admissions/financial-aid

ADDITIONAL INFORMATION:

Available Degree(s)

- B.A. Architecture

Portfolio Requirement

There is no portfolio requirement for first-year applicants. Students must submit a portfolio of work during their second year.

Scholarships Offered

Yale scholarships are grants that are solely need-based. Merit-based scholarships are funded by external organizations or private companies. Yale does not require students, whose parents earn less than $65,000 annually, to contribute toward educational costs. Students whose families earn more than $150,000 may qualify for financial aid.

Special Opportunities

Architecture students may choose a concentration in History, Theory, & Criticism, Design, or Urbanism. Additionally, architecture students may apply for the Harvey Geiger Fellowship which allows summer travel and research opportunities.

Notable Alumni

Albert Barokas, Edward D. Dart, Norman Foster, Brendon Gill, John Graham, Jr., Muzharul Islam, Johannes Knoops, Maya Lin, Herbert P. McLaughlin, Joshua Prince-Ramus, Richard Rogers, Eero Saarinen, Robert A. M. Stern, and Evans Woollen III

BOSTON ARCHITECTURAL COLLEGE

Address: 320 Newbury St., Boston, MA 02115
Website: *https://the-bac.edu/*
Contact: *https://the-bac.edu/about-the-bac/contact-us*
Phone: (617) 585-0100
Email: admissions@the-bac.edu

COST OF ATTENDANCE:

Tuition & Fees: $25,752 | **Additional Expenses:** $19,350
Total: $45,102

Financial Aid: https://the-bac.edu/admissions/financial-aid

ADDITIONAL INFORMATION:

Available Degree(s)
- Bachelor of Architecture (B.Arch.) - 5-year
- B.S. Architecture
- Bachelor of Interior Architecture
- Bachelor of Landscape Architecture (B.L.A.)

Graduate Degree(s)
- Master of Architecture (M.Arch.)
- Master of Interior Architecture
- Master of Landscape Architecture (M.L.A.)
- Master of Design Studies in Design for Human Health
- Master of Design Studies in Historic Preservation

Portfolio Requirement
Boston Architectural College has an open admissions policy. Portfolios are not required. However, applicants are strongly encouraged to submit one. Students without design experience are welcome to apply. Applicants without a portfolio are asked to complete a Work Sample instead of a portfolio. This entails submitting an example of creative work that reflects the applicant's personality. Submit all materials via WeTransfer.

Scholarships Offered
BAC offers several merit-based scholarships for students. Opportunities vary based on the type of architecture program. Awards range from $1,500-$2,600. Students must apply by the priority application deadline to be considered for the Dean's scholarship.

Special Opportunities
Boston Architectural College offers an advanced, online 2-year degree towards their B.S. in Architecture that leads to an accelerated 2-year Master of Architecture. This program is only available to transfer students. Additionally, architecture students are required to fulfill a work requirement, the Practice requirement, to graduate. By the time of graduation, most students will have full-time work experience at a design firm.

Notable Alumni
Edward F. Allodi, Arcangelo Cascieri, Charles L. Fletcher, Buckminster Fuller, Glenn Gissler, Wallace Harrison, William Sutherland Maxwell, Louis Skidmore, Edward Durell Stone, and Stewart Wurtz

CONNECTICUT

MAINE

MASSACHUSETTS

NEW HAMPSHIRE

NEW JERSEY

NEW YORK

PENNSYLVANIA

RHODE ISLAND

VERMONT

NORTHEAST

CONNECTICUT

MAINE

MASSACHUSETTS

NEW HAMPSHIRE

NEW JERSEY

NEW YORK

PENNSYLVANIA

RHODE ISLAND

VERMONT

HARVARD UNIVERSITY

Address: Harvard University, Cambridge, MA 02138
Website: *https://earlydesigneducation.gsd.harvard.edu/harvard-college-undergraduate-architecture-studies/*
Contact: *https://www.harvard.edu/contact-harvard*
Phone: (617) 495-1000
Email: Use contact form - https://college.harvard.edu/contact-us

COST OF ATTENDANCE:

Tuition & Fees: $55,587 | **Additional Expenses:** $23,341
Total: $78,928

Financial Aid: https://college.harvard.edu/financial-aid

ADDITIONAL INFORMATION:

Available Degree(s)

- A.B. in History of Art and Architecture

Graduate Degree(s)

- M.Arch., MLA, Master in Urban Planning,
- Master in Design Engineering
- Ph.D. Architecture, Landscape Architecture and Urban Planning
- Doctor of Design

Portfolio Requirement

Portfolios are not required, they are optional.

Scholarships Offered

Students pay only the remaining need after parent contribution and outside awards are covered by Harvard's scholarship funds. Students may also apply for external scholarships and grants. Harvard does not require students, whose parents earn less than $65,000 annually, to contribute toward educational costs. Students whose families earn more than $150,000 may qualify for financial aid. For most families, Harvard costs less than a public university. Students receive the same aid regardless of nationality or citizenship.

Special Opportunities

Students may study abroad, however, they must start this process early. Studying abroad requires speaking with the Director of Undergraduate Studies.

Notable Alumni

Barbara Bestor, Anna Campbell Bliss, Charles Bulfinch, Philip Johnson, Jarvis Hunt, Fumihiko Maki, Architect, I.M. Pei, and Henry Hobson Richardson

MASSACHUSETTS INSTITUTE OF TECHNOLOGY (MIT)

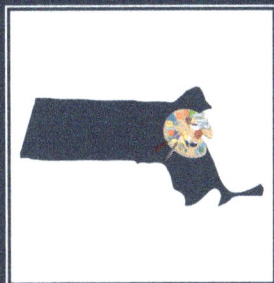

Address: 77 Massachusetts Ave, Cambridge, MA 02139
Website: *https://architecture.mit.edu/overview/undergraduate-degrees*
Contact: *https://web.mit.edu/contact/*
Phone: (617) 253-1000
Email: admissions@mit.edu

COST OF ATTENDANCE:

Tuition & Fees: $55,818 | **Additional Expenses:** $20,332
Total: $76,150

Financial Aid: https://sfs.mit.edu/undergraduate-students/

ADDITIONAL INFORMATION:

CONNECTICUT

MAINE

MASSACHUSETTS

NEW HAMPSHIRE

NEW JERSEY

NEW YORK

PENNSYLVANIA

RHODE ISLAND

VERMONT

Available Degree(s)

- B.S. Architecture
- B.S. Art & Design

Graduate Degree(s)

- Master of Architecture (M.Arch.)

Portfolio Requirement

None required. However, researchers, makers, and performing/ visual artists may submit an optional portfolio through SlideRoom. All media are accepted (up to 10 - design, drawing, painting, mixed media, digital media, photography, sculpture, and architecture work). MIT holds 30-120 minute admissions interviews with candidates if possible.

Scholarships Offered

MIT commits to meeting 100% of student's demonstrated need.

Special Opportunities

MIT offers a unique program, MITdesignX, which combines design innovation with entrepreneurship. Furthermore, they offer global teaching labs, exhibits, global startup labs, and internships.

Notable Alumni

Christopher Charles Benninger, Walter Danforth Bliss, Gordon Bunshaft, Ogden Codman, Jr., Vishaan Chakrabarti, John Desmond, Cass Gilbert, Charles Sumner Greene, Henry Mather Greene, Marion Mahony Griffin, Raymond Hood, Lois Lilley Howe, Jarvis Hunt, Myron Hunt, Roger K. Lewis, Austin W. Lord, I.M. Pei, Louis Sullivan, James Knox Taylor, Robert Taylor, and Harry Mohr Weese

NORTHEAST

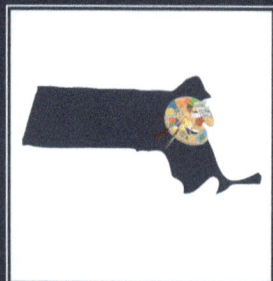

CONNECTICUT

MAINE

MASSACHUSETTS

NEW HAMPSHIRE

NEW JERSEY

NEW YORK

PENNSYLVANIA

RHODE ISLAND

VERMONT

NORTHEASTERN UNIVERSITY

Address: 360 Huntington Ave, Boston, MA 02115
Website: *https://camd.northeastern.edu/program/architecture-bs/*
Contact: *https://admissions.northeastern.edu/visit/contact/*
Phone: (617) 373-2200
Email: admissions@northeastern.edu

COST OF ATTENDANCE:

Tuition & Fees: $55,452 | **Additional Expenses:** $20,280
Total: $75,732

Financial Aid: https://studentfinance.northeastern.edu/

ADDITIONAL INFORMATION:

Available Degree(s)

- B.S. Architecture

Graduate Degree(s)

- Master of Architecture (M.Arch.)

Portfolio Requirement

Portfolios are optional. Students apply through the Common App or Coalition.

Scholarships Offered

Northeastern offers merit scholarships of $10,000-$20,000 annually for the Dean's Scholarship. CAMD Creative Leadership Scholarship awards $5,000-$20,000 annually. However, a portfolio is required to be considered for this award. Need-based scholarships are also offered.

Special Opportunities

Students take one additional year after the B.S. in Architecture to earn an M.Arch. Architecture students take studio classes, field study, student competitions, and workshops abroad. Furthermore, students may spend a semester studying in Segovia, Spain. Last, students complete two six-month co-ops; architectural studies or architectural design combined with civil engineering, environmental engineering, landscape architecture.

Notable Alumni

Eddie Alvarado, Laura Carlson, Shelly Chipimo, Juliet Chun, Christian Daff, Florencia Lima Gomez, Robert Levash, Laura Moss, Kelly Smith, and Filipe Tejeda

NEW JERSEY INSTITUTE OF TECHNOLOGY (NJIT)

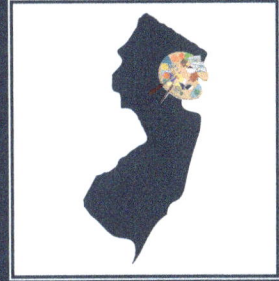

Address: Weston Hall 340, University Heights, Newark, NJ 07102
Website: *https://design.njit.edu/new-jersey-school-architecture*
Contact: *https://design.njit.edu/contact*
Phone: (973) 596-3080
Email: admissions@njit.edu

COST OF ATTENDANCE:

In-State Tuition & Fees: $18,016 | **Additional Expenses:** $23,700
Total: $41,716

Out-of-State Tuition & Fees: $34,034 | **Additional Expenses:** $23,700
Total: $57,734

Financial Aid: https://www5.njit.edu/financialaid/

ADDITIONAL INFORMATION:

Available Degree(s)

- Bachelor of Architecture (B.Arch.) - 5-year
- B.S. Architecture

Graduate Degree(s)

- Master of Architecture (M.Arch.)
- M.S. Architecture
- Master of Urban Design
- M.Arch. and Infrastructure Planning (M.I.P.)
- M.Arch. and Civil Engineering (M.S.)
- M.Arch. and Master of Business Administration (M.B.A.)
- Ph.D. Urban Systems

Portfolio Requirement

A portfolio of 10-20 examples of creative work is required. Submit via SlideRoom. Applicants are encouraged to supplement their portfolio with other samples of work, such as original music, creative writing, performance art, etc. Students are discouraged from copying characters from cartoons, television shows, or films.

Scholarships Offered

The College of Architecture and Design offers numerous awards based on leadership, service, academic achievement, and design excellence. Some awards are also need-based. Award amounts vary. NJIT also offers the Dean's Scholarship, a merit-based award that varies, based on academic achievement.

Special Opportunities

NJIT's B.Arch. is a five-year professional program, accredited by the National Architectural Accrediting Board (NAAB). B.Arch. students may specialize in Urbanism, Computation and Fabrication, or Sustainability. Furthermore, they may take dual degrees in the following areas: Infrastructure Planning, Construction Management, Civil Engineering, or Business Administration.

Notable Alumni

Mariam Abdelazim, Samuel Alemany, Mustafa Bahce, Sarah Kiczek, Catrina Nelson, and Oscar Villalobos

CONNECTICUT

MAINE

MASSACHUSETTS

NEW HAMPSHIRE

NEW JERSEY

NEW YORK

PENNSYLVANIA

RHODE ISLAND

VERMONT

NORTHEAST

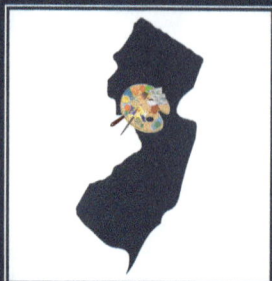

CONNECTICUT

MAINE

MASSACHUSETTS

NEW HAMPSHIRE

NEW JERSEY

NEW YORK

PENNSYLVANIA

RHODE ISLAND

VERMONT

PRINCETON UNIVERSITY

Address: Princeton University, Princeton, NJ 08544
Website: *https://soa.princeton.edu/content/undergraduate-program-architecture*
Contact: *https://admission.princeton.edu/contact-us*
Phone: (609) 258-3000
Email: uaoffice@princeton.edu

COST OF ATTENDANCE:

Tuition & Fees: $57,690 | **Additional Expenses:** $22,210
Total: $79,900

Financial Aid: https://admission.princeton.edu/cost-aid

ADDITIONAL INFORMATION:

Available Degree(s)

- A.B. with a concentration in Architecture

Portfolio Requirement

A portfolio is required. Media uploads can include images, video, 3D models, audio, or documents. Submit via SlideRoom after completing the university application.

Scholarships Offered

Financial aid is awarded solely based on need. There are no merit scholarships. For all families whose income is $65,000 or less, Princeton covers tuition, room, and board. Students whose parents earn less than $160,000 do not pay tuition. Students whose parents earn between $160,000 - $200,000 pay 79% to 95% tuition. For all students, whose parents early less than $65,000 per year do not pay for tuition, room, or board.

Special Opportunities

Architecture students participate in studio sessions with faculty T/Th for three hours per week. Furthermore, they may work towards one of two certificates, the Program in Urban Studies or the Program in Architecture and Engineering.

Notable Alumni

Stan Allen, Merritt Bucholz, Thomas S. Buechner, Elizabeth Diller, Michael Graves, Paul Lewis, Sergey Padyukov, Monica Ponce de Leon, Demetri Porphyrios, Kazuyo Sejima, William Turnbull, Jr. Robert Venturi, Sarah Whiting, and Marion Sims Wyeth

THE CITY COLLEGE OF NEW YORK - CUNY

Address: 141 Convent Avenue, New York, NY 10031
Website: *https://ssa.ccny.cuny.edu/*
Contact: *https://ssa.ccny.cuny.edu/about/contact/*
Phone: (212) 650-7118
Email: ssainfo@ccny.cuny.edu

COST OF ATTENDANCE:

In-State Tuition & Fees: $7,340 | **Additional Expenses:** $24,446
Total: $31,786

Out-of-State Tuition & Fees: $15,290 | **Additional Expenses:** $24,446
Total: $39,736

Financial Aid: https://ssa.ccny.cuny.edu/admissions/
undergraduate/ug-paying-for-school/

ADDITIONAL INFORMATION:

Available Degree(s)

- Bachelor of Architecture (B.Arch.) - 5-year
- B.S. Architectural Studies

Graduate Degree(s)

- Master of Architecture (M.Arch.)
- M.S. Architecture
- Master of Landscape Architecture (M.L.A.)
- Master of Urban Planning
- Master of Urban Sustainability

Portfolio Requirement

All students must complete the Creative Challenge. This challenge consists of a series of questions that the applicant must answer in the form of creative work. Students must scan their completed work and submit it via mail. Additional, traditional portfolios are only required for transfer applicants.

Scholarships Offered

Students must submit a separate application to be considered for scholarships. Students are encouraged to explore CUNY scholarships and external sources of aid.

Special Opportunities

Students have 24/7 studio access. In addition, the Solar Roofpod is a roof pavilion that provides green energy to urban buildings. It is a "hub for sustainable design" that is sometimes used as a classroom.

Notable Alumni

Mohammed Gueye, Gloria Hwoang, Atim Annette Oton, Evana Said, and Crystal Xing

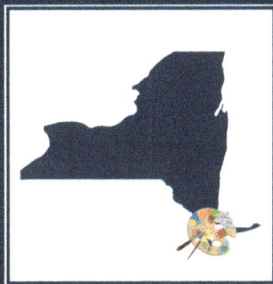

CONNECTICUT

MAINE

MASSACHUSETTS

NEW HAMPSHIRE

NEW JERSEY

NEW YORK

PENNSYLVANIA

RHODE ISLAND

VERMONT

NORTHEAST

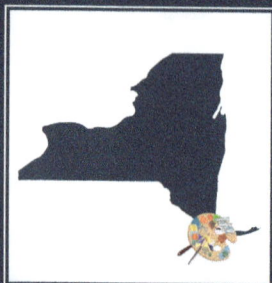

CONNECTICUT

MAINE

MASSACHUSETTS

NEW HAMPSHIRE

NEW JERSEY

NEW YORK

PENNSYLVANIA

RHODE ISLAND

VERMONT

THE COOPER UNION

Address: 30 Cooper Sq, New York, NY 10003
Website: *https://cooper.edu/architecture*
Contact: *https://cooper.edu/admissions/contact*
Phone: (212) 353-4120
Email: admissions@cooper.edu

COST OF ATTENDANCE:

Tuition & Fees: $46,820 | **Additional Expenses:** $22,302
Total: $69,122

Financial Aid: https://cooper.edu/admissions/financial-aid

ADDITIONAL INFORMATION:

Available Degree(s)

- Bachelor of Architecture (B.Arch.) - 5-year

Graduate Degree(s)

- M.S. Architecture

Portfolio Requirement

Cooper Union is on the Common App. Its supplemental application opens in September. Applicants must complete a Studio Test which appears in your applicant portal once the test is released.

Scholarships Offered

All accepted architecture students are offered generous $22,275 in scholarships for full-time students with the possibility of additional merit and need-based scholarships. There are also continuing scholarships.

Special Opportunities

Research and fellowship opportunities include Architecture Travel Fellowships, the Thesis Fellowship, the Innovation Fellowship, weekly eBulletin, books of works, the Center for Urban Infrastructure, and various field trips. With a goal to synthesize social, aesthetic, and technological aspects of architecture, the university provides studios, computer access, an Art & Architecture Shop (wood, metal, plastics, clay, and bronze casting foundry), 3D printing, laser cutting, modeling/rendering, and rapid prototype machines.

Notable Alumni

Stan Alen, Karen Bausman, Architect, William Francis Deegan, Olvia C. Demetrious, Elizabeth Diller, Brad Friedmutter, Lenora Garfinkel, T.J. Gottesdiener, John Hejduk, Thomas W. Lamb, Daniel Libeskind, Toshiko Mori, Michel Mossesian, Victor Nellenbogen, Eleanore Pettersen, Ron Pompei, Edward Sargent, Ricardo Scofidio, and Charles B.J. Snyder

CORNELL UNIVERSITY

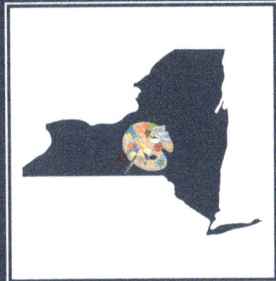

Address: 139 Sibley Dome, Cornell University, Ithaca, NY 14853
Website: *https://aap.cornell.edu/*
Contact: *https://aap.cornell.edu/about/contact*
Phone: (607) 255-5236
Email: cuarch@cornell.edu

COST OF ATTENDANCE:

Tuition & Fees: $60,285 | **Additional Expenses:** $16,396
Total: $76,681

Financial Aid: https://finaid.cornell.edu/

ADDITIONAL INFORMATION:

Available Degree(s)

- Bachelor of Architecture (B.Arch.) - 5-year

Portfolio Requirement

Prospective B.Arch. students must request a portfolio interview with a professor or alum and present artwork samples. Portfolios must contain 15-20 slides and have carefully crafted captions, submitted via SlideRoom. Include freehand drawings and a range of artistic media.

Scholarships Offered

Nine scholarships are offered each year specifically for architecture students. Cornell offers the Future Architect Award for underrepresented students. Cornell guarantees that any family with a total income of less than $60,000, and total assets of less than $100,000 (including primary home equity), will have no parent contribution and no loans.

Special Opportunities

B.Arch. students study history, theory, and practice with a choice of the following concentrations: Architecture, Culture, and Society; Architecture Science and Technology; History of Architecture; Architectural Analysis; Visual Representation in Architecture. Cornell's Summer Architecture Program focuses on design, practice, lectures, workshops, portfolio review, and field trips. As one of the oldest architecture programs in the U.S., there is a large alumni network.

Additionally, Cornell houses specialized studio spaces such as the L.P. Kwee Studios and Frances Shloss Studio, as well as Fabrication Shops, Photography Labs, Darkrooms, and Print Media Facilities. Students present in exhibitions in the Bibliowicz Family Gallery, John Hartell Gallery, Sibley Exhibition Hallway, and Olive Tjaden Gallery, and Experimental Gallery.

Notable Alumni

Albert Cassell, Peter Eisenman, Raymond M. Kennedy, Rem Koolhaas, Tomas Mapua, Richard Meier, Lawrence Perkins, Frederick Roehrig, Richmond Shreve, Helen Binkerd Young, and Ricardo Zurita

CONNECTICUT

MAINE

MASSACHUSETTS

NEW HAMPSHIRE

NEW JERSEY

NEW YORK

PENNSYLVANIA

RHODE ISLAND

VERMONT

NORTHEAST

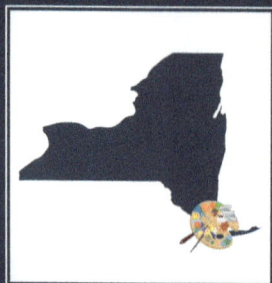

CONNECTICUT

MAINE

MASSACHUSETTS

NEW HAMPSHIRE

NEW JERSEY

NEW YORK

PENNSYLVANIA

RHODE ISLAND

VERMONT

NEW YORK INSTITUTE OF TECHNOLOGY (NYIT)

Address: 1855 Broadway, New York, NY 10023
Website: *https://www.nyit.edu/architecture*
Contact: *https://www.nyit.edu/architecture/contact*
Phone: (212) 261-1629
Email: nyitarch@nyit.edu
Other locations: Long Island, NY

COST OF ATTENDANCE:

Tuition & Fees: $42,360 | **Additional Expenses:** $16,085
Total: $58,445

Financial Aid: https://www.nyit.edu/admissions/financial_aid

ADDITIONAL INFORMATION:

Available Degree(s)

- Bachelor of Architecture (B.Arch.) - 5-year
- B.S. Architectural Technology, (B.S.A.T.) concentrations: Construction Management

Graduate Degree(s)

- Master of Architecture (M.Arch.)
- M.S. Architecture, Health and Design
- M.S. Architecture, Computational Technologies
- M.S. Architecture, Urban Design

Portfolio Requirement

A portfolio is required for entry to the B.Arch. Students must submit 10-15 pages of visual work. Applicants who are not admitted to the B.Arch. as first-years will be automatically considered for the B.S.A.T. program.

Scholarships Offered

NYIT offers several academic scholarships, including the President's Scholarship ($25,000), Theodore K. Steele Memorial Scholarship ($22,000), and more.

Special Opportunities

Applicants may apply directly into the B.Arch. program or, if not accepted, the applicant will be automatically considered for the B.S.A.T. program and may apply to the B.Arch. program in their third year.

Notable Alumni

Matthew Acer, Arianna Armelli, Joseph Fuller, and Roger P. Smith

PRATT INSTITUTE

Address: 200 Willoughby Avenue, Brooklyn, NY 11205
Website: *https://www.pratt.edu/academics/architecture/*
Contact: *https://www.pratt.edu/academics/architecture/school-of-architecture-contact/*
Phone: (718) 636-3600
Email: admissions@pratt.edu

COST OF ATTENDANCE:

Tuition & Fees: $53,566 | **Additional Expenses:** $19,824
Total: $73,390

Financial Aid: https://www.pratt.edu/admissions/financing-your-education/financing-undergraduate/

ADDITIONAL INFORMATION:

Available Degree(s)

- Bachelor of Architecture (B.Arch.) - 5-year
- B.S. Construction Management

Graduate Degree(s)

- Master of Architecture (M.Arch.)
- M.S. Architecture

Portfolio Requirement

Pratt requires a SlideRoom portfolio for all majors except construction management. Applicants must submit 12-20 pieces of their best work (variety – paintings, drawings, sculpture, ceramics, etc.). Of the works submitted, 3-5 must be observational drawings (e.g., landscape, still-life, self-portrait, figure, or interior spaces).

Scholarships Offered

Pratt Institute offers various merit-based scholarships. About 78% of Pratt students receive some form of aid.

Special Opportunities

Students may study abroad in the Berlin or China Summer Programs. Furthermore, Pratt has special programs in Construction Management, Facilities Management, Real Estate Practice, Graduate Architecture & Urban Design, Planning & Development, and the Center for Experimental Structures. Architecture students may also minor in Morphology.

Notable Alumni

Joe Amisano, Ralph Appelbaum, Charles Belfoure, Guy Bolton, Elizabeth Crowley, Johannes Knoops, Henry F. Ludorf, Elisabeth Martini, Henry V. Murphy, J. Gerald Phelan, John M. Pierce, George Ranalli, Annabelle Selldorf, William Van Alen, Carlos Zapata, and Peter Zumthor

CONNECTICUT

MAINE

MASSACHUSETTS

NEW HAMPSHIRE

NEW JERSEY

NEW YORK

PENNSYLVANIA

RHODE ISLAND

VERMONT

NORTHEAST

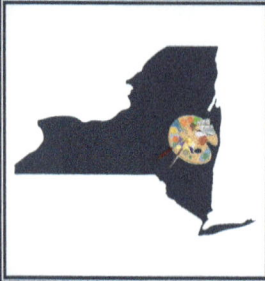

CONNECTICUT

MAINE

MASSACHUSETTS

NEW HAMPSHIRE

NEW JERSEY

NEW YORK

PENNSYLVANIA

RHODE ISLAND

VERMONT

RENSSELAER POLYTECHNIC INSTITUTE (RPI)

Address: 110 8th Street, Troy, NY 12180
Website: *https://www.arch.rpi.edu/*
Contact: *https://info.rpi.edu/contactus*
Phone: (518) 276-6877
Email: admissions@rpi.edu

COST OF ATTENDANCE:

Tuition & Fees: $58,526 | **Additional Expenses:** $19,237
Total: $77,763

Financial Aid: https://admissions.rpi.edu/aid/

ADDITIONAL INFORMATION:

Available Degree(s)

- Bachelor of Architecture (B.Arch.) - 5-year
- B.S. Building Sciences

Portfolio Requirement

Applicants must submit a portfolio via SlideRoom. Portfolios include 10-20 images of work in a range of media. Admissions prefers that applicants do not include architectural drafted drawings.

Scholarships Offered

RPI offers several types of merit scholarships for students. The Rensselaer Medal Award is valued at $30,000 per year and guaranteed for all five years of the B.Arch. program.

Special Opportunities

The Arch Semester Away, a study abroad work experience open to fourth year students.

Notable Alumni

Peter Bohlin, Charles Amos Cummings, and Steven Ehrlich

SUNY COLLEGE OF TECHNOLOGY AT ALFRED STATE UNIVERSITY

Address: 10 Upper College Dr., Alfred, NY 14802
Website: *https://www.alfredstate.edu/architecture*
Contact: *https://catalog.alfredstate.edu/current/campus-telephone-directory.php*
Phone: (607) 587-4064

COST OF ATTENDANCE:

In-State Tuition & Fees: $8,862 | **Additional Expenses:** $13,450
Total: $22,312

Out-of-State Tuition & Fees: $18,772 | **Additional Expenses:** $13,450
Total: $32,222

Financial Aid: https://www.alfredstate.edu/financial-aid

ADDITIONAL INFORMATION:

Available Degree(s)

- Bachelor of Architecture (B.Arch.) - 5-year
- B.S. Architectural Technology

Portfolio Requirement

Applicants for the B.Arch. must submit a portfolio via SlideRoom. Portfolios must include 10-20 examples of the student's best work. Applicants of the B.S. listed here are not required to submit a portfolio.

Scholarships Offered

SUNY at Alfred offers the academic distinction award, valued at $4,000 along with other need-based and merit-based scholarships.

Special Opportunities

Students may participate in study abroad, leadership opportunities through the AIAS, field study trips, access to the Center for Architecture & Remote Sensing, and a field study experience opportunities with Historicorps.

Notable Alumni

Robert Steen, Peter Trowbridge, and Hannah Weaver

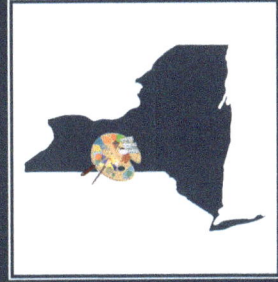

CONNECTICUT

MAINE

MASSACHUSETTS

NEW HAMPSHIRE

NEW JERSEY

NEW YORK

PENNSYLVANIA

RHODE ISLAND

VERMONT

NORTHEAST

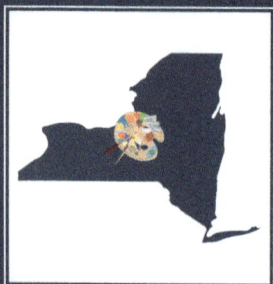

CONNECTICUT

MAINE

MASSACHUSETTS

NEW HAMPSHIRE

NEW JERSEY

NEW YORK

PENNSYLVANIA

RHODE ISLAND

VERMONT

ME
VT
NY
NH
MA
PA
RI
CT
NJ

SYRACUSE UNIVERSITY

Address: 201 Slocum Hall, Syracuse, NY 13244
Website: *https://soa.syr.edu/*
Contact: *https://soa.syr.edu/contact-us/*
Phone: (315) 443-2256
Email: orange@syr.edu

COST OF ATTENDANCE:

Tuition & Fees: $55,920 | **Additional Expenses:** $24,119
Total: $80,039

Financial Aid: https://www.syracuse.edu/admissions/cost-and-aid/

ADDITIONAL INFORMATION:

Available Degree(s)

- Bachelor of Architecture (B.Arch.) - 5-year

Portfolio Requirement

Applicants must submit a portfolio via SlideRoom, in person, or by mail. Portfolios should include 12-24 reproductions of the student's best and most recent work, all labeled and with a 1-2 sentence caption. Works from observation are highly encouraged. Mechanical/architectural drawings are accepted. However, they will be evaluated based on artistic merit, not on manipulation of software.

Scholarships Offered

Syracuse University offers various merit-based and need-based scholarships and grants. The 1870 Scholarship covers full tuition for the full length of the undergraduate program.

Special Opportunities

Students have the opportunity to study abroad. More than 90% of architecture students study abroad at some point during their time at Syracuse University.

Notable Alumni

Dean Alvord, Harley Baldwin, Thomas Boyde, Jr., Lori Brown, Massimo Carmassi, Arthur Bridgman Clark, Bruce Fowle, James Garrison, Adam Gross, Wilbur R. Ingalls, Jr. Lorimer Rich, David Rockwell, and Werner Seligmann

CARNEGIE MELLON UNIVERSITY

Address: 5000 Forbes Avenue, Pittsburgh, PA 15213
Website: *https://soa.cmu.edu/*
Contact: *https://admission.enrollment.cmu.edu/pages/contact-us*
Phone: (412) 268-2354
Email: admission@andrew.cmu.edu

COST OF ATTENDANCE:

Tuition & Fees: $57,560 | **Additional Expenses:** $19,914
Total: $77,474

Financial Aid: https://www.cmu.edu/admission/aid-affordability

ADDITIONAL INFORMATION:

Available Degree(s)

- Bachelor of Architecture (B.Arch.) - 5-year
- B.A. Architecture
- BXA Intercollege Degree

Portfolio Requirement

All 3 programs require a SlideRoom portfolio. Applicants must submit 10 creative works. Students must also register to participate in an online formal portfolio review to SlideRoom (one-on-one w/ faculty via Zoom; not required, but strongly recommended.)

Scholarships Offered

CMU offers a need-based grant and endowed scholarships. Undergrad, graduate, and alumni awards are available as well. Current students can win design, sustainability, research, and engagement scholarships ($75,000 additional awarded each year).

Special Opportunities

Sustainable, computational, and urban design opportunities are available through the Applied Architectural Robotics Collective (AARC), the Center for Building and Performance Diagnostics (CBPD), the Computational Design Lab (Code Lab), the Remaking Cities Institute (RCI) with government, industry, and nonprofit partners.

Students may also participate in the EX-CHANGE exhibition and publication, apply for the $12,000 Delbert Highlands Travel Fellowship and participate in the Freedom By Design community service program with AIAS. Furthermore, CMU offers exchange programs with the National University of Singapore and Ecole Polytechnique Fédérale de Lausanne (EPFL) and Architecture Summer Study Abroad Studios, all taught by CMU faculty.

Notable Alumni

Nader Ardalan, Roger Duffy, and Steven Song

CONNECTICUT

MAINE

MASSACHUSETTS

NEW HAMPSHIRE

NEW JERSEY

NEW YORK

PENNSYLVANIA

RHODE ISLAND

VERMONT

NORTHEAST

CONNECTICUT

MAINE

MASSACHUSETTS

NEW HAMPSHIRE

NEW JERSEY

NEW YORK

PENNSYLVANIA

RHODE ISLAND

VERMONT

PENN STATE UNIVERSITY (PENN STATE)

Address: 124 Borland Building, University Park, PA 16802
Website: *https://arts.psu.edu/*
Contact: *https://admissions.psu.edu/contact/*
Phone: (814) 865-2591
Email: admissions@psu.edu

COST OF ATTENDANCE:

In-State Tuition & Fees: $18,898 | **Additional Expenses:** $14,158
Total: $33,056

Out-of-State Tuition & Fees: $36,476 | **Additional Expenses:** $14,158
Total: $50,634

Financial Aid: https://studentaid.psu.edu/

ADDITIONAL INFORMATION:

Available Degree(s)

- Bachelor of Architecture (B.Arch.) - 5-year

Graduate Degree(s)

- Master of Architecture (M.Arch.)
- M.S. Architecture
- Dual M.S. Architecture and HDNRE
- Ph.D. Architecture
- Dual Ph.D. Architecture and HDNRE

Portfolio Requirement

There is no portfolio requirement for incoming first year students. The portfolio is required for a student within Penn State who is changing their major, or for transfer students.

Scholarships Offered

Penn State offers various university scholarships with awards up to $7,000 per year.

Special Opportunities

Architecture students are required to participate in a semester of study abroad in Rome, Copenhagen, or Korea/Japan. Furthermore, the M.S. and Ph.D. programs offer dual degrees with the Human Dimensions of Natural Resources and the Environment program (HDNRE). This intercollege program allows students to study global climate change and sustainable design.

Notable Alumni

Louis D. Astorino and Stanley Cole

THOMAS JEFFERSON UNIVERSITY

Address: 4201 Henry Avenue, Philadelphia, PA 19144
Website: *https://www.jefferson.edu/academics/colleges-schools-institutes/architecture-and-the-built-environment.html*
Contact: *https://www.jefferson.edu/academics/colleges-schools-institutes/architecture-and-the-built-environment/about/contact-request-info.html*
Phone: (215) 951-2800
Email: Admissions@PhilaU.edu

COST OF ATTENDANCE:

Tuition & Fees: $42,966 | **Additional Expenses:** $14,949
Total: $57,925

Financial Aid: https://www.jefferson.edu/tuition-and-financial-aid.html

ADDITIONAL INFORMATION:

Available Degree(s)

- Bachelor of Architecture (B.Arch.) - 5-year
- B.S. Architectural Studies
- B.S. Construction Management
- B.S. Interior Design
- Bachelor of Landscape Architecture (B.L.A.)

Graduate Degree(s)

- Master of Architecture (M.Arch.)
- M.S. Architecture
- M.S. Construction Management
- M.S. Geospatial Technology for Geodesign
- M.S. Historic PReservation
- M.S. Interior Architecture
- M.S. Real Estate Development
- M.S. Sustainable Design
- Master of Urban Design (M.U.D.)

Portfolio Requirement

Portfolios are optional for first-year applicants. Only transfer students are required to submit one. Portfolios must be submitted via SlideRoom and include at least 12 works. Applicants should include drawings from observation, computer-aided design work, form explorations, and evidence of problem-solving.

Scholarships Offered

Thomas Jefferson University offers various merit-based, athletic, and endowed scholarships. Merit awards range from $4,000 to $19,000 for incoming freshmen.

Special Opportunities

Students may study abroad during their fourth year of study. Two locations are available: the University of Arkansas Rome Center (UARC) or the Danish Institute for Study Abroad in Copenhagen. Furthermore, students may opt for a 5-year B.S. in Interior Design/M.S. in Sustainable Design, the 5+1 B.S. in Architecture and M.S. in Real Estate Development, the 4+1 B.L.A./M.S. in Geodesign, and other opportunities.

Notable Alumni

Amy Hufford, Crystal Russell, Ghislaine Viñas, and Kim Wannop

CONNECTICUT

MAINE

MASSACHUSETTS

NEW HAMPSHIRE

NEW JERSEY

NEW YORK

PENNSYLVANIA

RHODE ISLAND

VERMONT

NORTHEAST

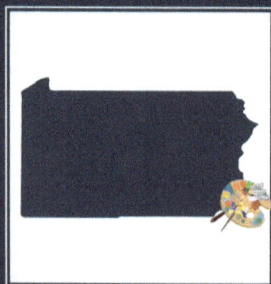

CONNECTICUT

MAINE

MASSACHUSETTS

NEW HAMPSHIRE

NEW JERSEY

NEW YORK

PENNSYLVANIA

RHODE ISLAND

VERMONT

UNIVERSITY OF PENNSYLVANIA

Address: University of Pennsylvania, Philadelphia, PA 19104
Website: *https://www.design.upenn.edu/architecture/undergraduate/about*
Contact: *https://www.design.upenn.edu/contact-us/university-pennsylvania-stuart-weitzman-school-design-offices*
Phone: (215) 573-5134
Email: admissions@design.upenn.edu

COST OF ATTENDANCE:

Tuition & Fees: $63,452 | **Additional Expenses:** $22,286
Total: $85,738

Financial Aid: https://srfs.upenn.edu/financial-aid/undergraduate-aid-program

ADDITIONAL INFORMATION:

Available Degree(s)

- B.A. Architecture

Graduate Degree(s)

- Master of Architecture (M.Arch.)
- Master of City Planning
- Master of Landscape Architecture (M.L.A.)
- Master of Environmental Building Design
- Master of Urban Spatial Analytics
- M.S. Architecture
- M.S. Design: Advanced Architectural Design (M.S.D.-A.A.D.)
- M.S. Design: Environmental Building Design (M.S.D.-E.B.D.)
- M.S. Design: Historic Preservation
- M.S. Design: Robotics and Autonomous Systems (M.S.D.-R.A.S.)
- M.S. Historic Preservation
- Ph.D. Architecture
- Ph.D. City and Regional Planning

Portfolio Requirement
There is no portfolio requirement for first-year applicants. However, transfer students must submit a portfolio.

Scholarships Offered
Named Scholarships, Penn Grants, the Mayor's Scholarship, and the Maguire Scholarship are available to all UPenn students. UPenn does not require students, whose parents earn less than $65,000 annually, to contribute toward educational costs.

Special Opportunities
High school students may apply for the Architecture Summer at Penn (ASAP) program. Architecture students at UPenn may enjoy the study abroad program in the Architectural Association (AA) in London, a Minor in Landscape Studies, or a concentration in Architecture Practice and Technology. Furthermore, UPenn offers an Integrated Product Design fundamentals course. Additionally, UPenn offers numerous dual degrees within the School of Design and across other Schools at UPenn.

Notable Alumni
Faris Al-Shathir, Abdulla A. Al Shamsi, E. Cecil Baker, William W. Braham III, Yu-Chieh Chiang, David G. De Long, Terry Farrell, John R. Hoke, Young Kyoon Jeong, Vanessa Keith, Stephen J. Kieran, Michael A. Kihn, A. Eugene Kohn, Susan Abel Maxman, Julie Torres Mshkovitz, Adele Naude Santos, Denise Scott Brown, Liang Sicheng, and Henry Smith-Miller

RHODE ISLAND SCHOOL OF DESIGN (RISD)

Address: 2 College St, Providence, RI 02903
Website: *https://www.risd.edu/academics/architecture/*
Contact: *https://www.risd.edu/academics/architecture/contact/*
Phone: (401) 454-6300
Email: admissions@risd.edu

COST OF ATTENDANCE:

Tuition & Fees: $55,220 | **Additional Expenses:** $22,060
Total: $77,280

Financial Aid: https://www.risd.edu/student-financial-services/undergraduate-aid/

ADDITIONAL INFORMATION:

Available Degree(s)

- Bachelor of Architecture (B.Arch.) - 5-year

Portfolio Requirement

Students present 12-20 of recent work submitted through SlideRoom. Include finished pieces, drawings from direct observation, and no more than three pieces that show research/prep work. Curate/edit pieces in your portfolio.

Scholarships Offered

RISD scholarships are need-based. Students must submit a FAFSA application each year to be considered. RISD is also partnered with Scholarship Universe, a website that matches students with outside scholarships and keeps students on track with deadlines.

Special Opportunities

Students can cross-register at Brown University at no extra cost. Architecture students may enjoy any of the Off-Campus-International Programs in Italy, France, or the UK. Furthermore, Wintersession courses include Mexico: Material Propositions: Oaxaca, Architectonics, Wearable Studio, Storytelling as a Space for Meditation.

Notable Alumni

Raed Abillama, Deborah Berke, Preston Scott Cohen, Jonathan L. Foote, Frances Henley, Allan Merrick Jeffers, Bernard Khoury, Richard Levine, Alice Malhiot, Michael Maltzan, Sam Posey, Ira Rakatansky, Hashim Sarkis, Richard M. Sommer, Nader Tehrani, Veronika Valk, and Clifford Wlens

CONNECTICUT

MAINE

MASSACHUSETTS

NEW HAMPSHIRE

NEW JERSEY

NEW YORK

PENNSYLVANIA

RHODE ISLAND

VERMONT

NORTHEAST

ILLINOIS

INDIANA

IOWA

KANSAS

MICHIGAN

MINNESOTA

MISSOURI

NEBRASKA

NORTH DAKOTA

OHIO

SOUTH DAKOTA

WISCONSIN

CHAPTER 12

REGION TWO

MIDWEST

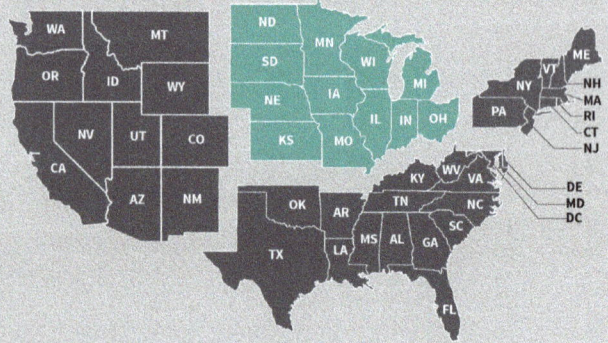

7 Programs | 12 States

1. IL – Illinois Institute of Technology
2. IL - University of Illinois Urbana-
   Champaign (UIUC)
3. IN - University of Notre Dame
4. IA - Iowa State University
5. MI - University of Michigan
6. MN - University of Minnesota
7. MO - Washington University in St. Louis

School	Avg. GPA, SAT Evidence-Based Reading Writing (ERW), SAT Math (M), and ACT Composite (C) Early Decision (ED): Yes/No	Admission Statistics	Program(s)	Portfolio Required (req.)
Illinois Institute of Technology 3360 South State Street, Chicago, IL 60616	GPA: N/A SAT (ERW): 570-670 SAT (M): 620-730 ACT (C): 26-32 ED: No	Overall College Admit Rate: 61% Undergrad Enrollment: 3,122 Total Enrollment: 6,325	Bachelor of Architecture (B.Arch.) - 5-year Graduate Degree(s): Master of Architecture (M.Arch.) Master of Landscape Architecture (M.L.A.) Masters of Tall Buildings & Vertical Urbanism Ph.D. Architecture Degrees Awarded in the Program(s): 55	Portfolio not req.
University of Illinois Urbana-Champaign (UIUC) 901 West Illinois Street, Urbana, IL 61801	GPA: N/A SAT (ERW): 590-700 SAT (M): 620-770 ACT (C): 27-33 ED: No	Overall College Admit Rate: 50% Undergrad Enrollment: 34,559 Total Enrollment: 56,257	B.S. Architectural Studies (B.S.A.S.) Graduate Degree(s): Master of Architecture (M.Arch.) M.S. Architectural Studies Degrees Awarded in the Program(s): 91	Portfolio not req.

School	Avg. GPA, SAT Evidence-Based Reading Writing (ERW), SAT Math (M), and ACT Composite (C) Early Decision (ED): Yes/No	Admission Statistics	Program(s)	Portfolio Required (req.)
University of Notre Dame 114 Walsh Family Hall of Architecture, Notre Dame, IN 46556	GPA: N/A SAT (ERW): 690-760 SAT (M): 710-790 ACT (C): 32-35 ED: No, but Restrictive Early Action (REA) available	Overall College Admit Rate: 19% Undergrad Enrollment: 8,874 Total Enrollment: 12,809	Bachelor of Architecture (B.Arch.) - 5-year Graduate Degree(s): Master of Architectural Design and Urbanism (M.ADU) Master of Architecture (M.Arch.) M.S. Historic Preservation (M.S.H.P.) Degrees Awarded in the Program(s): 36	Portfolio optional

MIDWEST

ARCHITECTURE PROGRAMS

School	Avg. GPA, SAT Evidence-Based Reading Writing (ERW), SAT Math (M), and ACT Composite (C) Early Decision (ED): Yes/No	Admission Statistics	Program(s)	Portfolio Required (req.)
Iowa State University 715 Bissell Rd, Ames, IA 50011	GPA: 3.71 SAT (ERW): 480-630 SAT (M): 530-680 ACT (C): 21-28 ED: No	Overall College Admit Rate: 88% Undergrad Enrollment: 26,843 Total Enrollment: 31,822	Bachelor of Architecture (B.Arch.) - 5-year Bachelor of Landscape Architecture (B.L.A.) Graduate Degree(s): Master of Architecture (M.Arch.) M.S. Architecture Degrees Awarded in the Program(s): 134	Portfolio not req.
University of Michigan 500 S. State St., Ann Arbor, MI 48109	GPA: 3.87 SAT (ERW): 660-740 SAT (M): 680-780 ACT (C): 31-34 ED: No	Overall College Admit Rate: 26% Undergrad Enrollment: 31,329 Total Enrollment: 47,907	B.S. Architecture Graduate Degree(s): Master of Architecture (M.Arch.) Master of Urban Design (M.U.D.) M.S. Architecture Ph.D. Architecture Degrees Awarded in the Program(s): 70	Portfolio req.

ARCHITECTURE PROGRAMS

School	Avg. GPA, SAT Evidence-Based Reading Writing (ERW), SAT Math (M), and ACT Composite (C) Early Decision (ED): Yes/No	Admission Statistics	Program(s)	Portfolio Required (req.)
University of Minnesota 330 21st Ave S., Minneapolis, MN 55455	GPA: N/A SAT (ERW): 600-700 SAT (M): 640-760 ACT (C): 25-31 ED: No	Overall College Admit Rate: 70% Undergrad Enrollment: 36,061 Total Enrollment: 52,017	B.S. Architecture Bachelor of Design in Architecture (B.D.A.) Graduate Degree(s): Master of Architecture (M.Arch.) Master of Heritage Studies and Public History M.S. Architecture, tracks: Sustainable Design; Metropolitan Design; Research Practices Ph.D. Design: Architecture Degrees Awarded in the Program(s): 117	Portfolio not req.

MIDWEST

ARCHITECTURE PROGRAMS

School	Avg. GPA, SAT Evidence-Based Reading Writing (ERW), SAT Math (M), and ACT Composite (C) Early Decision (ED): Yes/No	Admission Statistics	Program(s)	Portfolio Required (req.)
Washington University in St. Louis 1 Brookings Dr, St. Louis, MO 63130	GPA: 4.21 SAT (ERW): 720-760 SAT (M): 760-800 ACT (C): 33-35 ED: Yes	Overall College Admit Rate: 16% Undergrad Enrollment: 7,653 Total Enrollment: 15,449	B.A. Architecture B.S. Architecture Graduate Degree(s): Master of Architecture (M.Arch.) Master of Landscape Architecture (M.L.A.) Master of Urban Design (M.U.D.) M.S. Advanced Architectural Design M.S. Architectural Studies Doctor of Sustainable Urbanism (DrSU) Degrees Awarded in the Program(s): 39	Portfolio optional

ILLINOIS

INDIANA

IOWA

KANSAS

MICHIGAN

MINNESOTA

MISSOURI

NEBRASKA

NORTH DAKOTA

OHIO

SOUTH DAKOTA

WISCONSIN

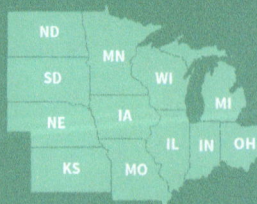

ILLINOIS INSTITUTE OF TECHNOLOGY

Address: 3360 South State Street, Chicago, IL 60616
Website: *http://arch.iit.edu/*
Contact: *http://arch.iit.edu/contact*
Phone: (312) 567-3230
Email: arch@iit.edu

COST OF ATTENDANCE:

Tuition & Fees: $50,640 | **Additional Expenses:** $15,570
Total: $66,210

Financial Aid: https://web.iit.edu/financial-aid/

ADDITIONAL INFORMATION:

Available Degree(s)

- Bachelor of Architecture (B.Arch.) - 5-year

Graduate Degree(s)

- Master of Architecture (M.Arch.)
- Master of Landscape Architecture (M.L.A.)
- Masters of Tall Buildings & Vertical Urbanism
- Ph.D. Architecture

Portfolio Requirement

Portfolio only required for transfer students and must be sent digitally via email. Transfer portfolio PDF should tell a compelling story about yourself, interests, and motivation to study architecture; compile visual work, images, drawings, and photos.

Scholarships Offered

The Crown Scholarship offers full tuition for five years for full-time architecture students. This scholarship is only available to first-year domestic students. In addition, other merit-based scholarships are available to students, such as the Camras Scholars Program (full tuition), Duchossois Leadership Scholars Program (full tuition, room, & board), etc.

Special Opportunities

Paid ten-week summer internships are available to IIT students only at certain Chicago architectural firms. In addition, B.Arch. students may consider the co-terminal program, where an extra year is added so the student may earn their M.Arch. There is also a 1-week architecture program available for middle school students. As for facilities, IIT houses one of the nation's largest fabrication labs.

Notable Alumni

Charles Draper Faulkner, Helmut Jahn, James Ingo Freed, Hans Hollein, Gertrude Kerbis, Florence Knoll, Phyllis Lambert, Howard Lane, Edward Noonan, Brigitte Peterhans, and Robert Bruce Tague

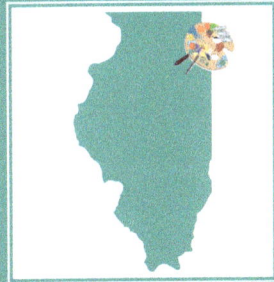

UNIVERSITY OF ILLINOIS URBANA-CHAMPAIGN (UIUC)

Address: 901 West Illinois Street, Urbana, IL 61801
Website: *https://arch.illinois.edu/programs-applying/
undergraduate-degrees/bachelor-of-science/*
Contact: *https://admissions.illinois.edu/contact*
Phone: (217) 333-0302
Email: admissions@illinois.edu

COST OF ATTENDANCE:

In-State Tuition & Fees: $16,866 | **Additional Expenses:** $16,194
Total: $33,060

Out-of-State Tuition & Fees: $34,316 | **Additional Expenses:** $16,534
Total: $50,850

Financial Aid: https://admissions.illinois.edu/Invest/financial-aid

ADDITIONAL INFORMATION:

Available Degree(s)

- B.S. Architectural Studies (B.S.A.S.)

Graduate Degree(s)

- Master of Architecture (M.Arch.)
- M.S. Architectural Studies

Portfolio Requirement

There is no portfolio requirement.

Scholarships Offered

Both in-state and out-of-state applicants are eligible for various
scholarships. College of Fine & Applied Arts talent-based awards
during their audition, interview, and/or portfolio review.

Special Opportunities

Study abroad is a popular option for architecture students.
Students may learn about Barcelona's unique architecture by
joining the immersive, year-long program in Barcelona, Spain.
UIUC also offers a Munich Exchange and a Stockholm Exchange for
one semester. UIUC offers numerous joint graduate degrees such
as the M.Arch. + Master of Urban Planning (M.U.P.), the M.Arch. +
M.S. Architectural Studies, and the M.Arch. + M.S. Civil Engineering
(M.S.C.E.).

Notable Alumni

Max Abramovitz, Henry Bacon, Clarence Blackall, Temple Hoyne
Buell, Alfred T. Fellheimer, Jeanne Gang, Ralph Johnson, David
Miller, Cesar Pelli, William Pereira, Alberta Pfeiffer, Nathan Clifford
Ricker, Carol Ross Barney, and Lebbeus Woods

ILLINOIS

INDIANA

IOWA

KANSAS

MICHIGAN

MINNESOTA

MISSOURI

NEBRASKA

NORTH DAKOTA

OHIO

SOUTH DAKOTA

WISCONSIN

MIDWEST

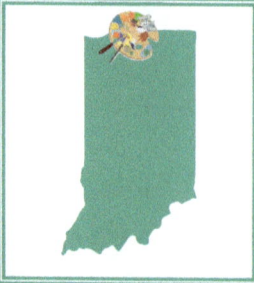

ILLINOIS

INDIANA

IOWA

KANSAS

MICHIGAN

MINNESOTA

MISSOURI

NEBRASKA

NORTH DAKOTA

OHIO

SOUTH DAKOTA

WISCONSIN

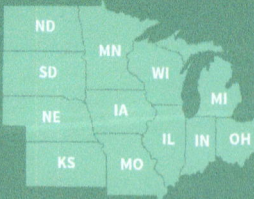

UNIVERSITY OF NOTRE DAME

Address: 114 Walsh Family Hall of Architecture, Notre Dame, IN 46556
Website: *https://architecture.nd.edu/*
Contact: *https://architecture.nd.edu/about/contact/*
Phone: (574) 631-6137
Email: arch@nd.edu

COST OF ATTENDANCE:

Tuition & Fees: $57,699 | **Additional Expenses:** $19,184
Total: $76,883

Financial Aid: https://financialaid.nd.edu/

ADDITIONAL INFORMATION:

Available Degree(s)

- Bachelor of Architecture (B.Arch.) - 5-year

Graduate Degree(s)

- Master of Architectural Design and Urbanism (M.ADU)
- Master of Architecture (M.Arch.)
- M.S. Historic Preservation (M.S.H.P.)

Portfolio Requirement

Portfolios are optional. Submit via SlideRoom. If submitting one, the applicant should include 12 works showcasing breadth in terms of media, subject, and color form.

Scholarships Offered

Notre Dame offers institutional scholarships, club scholarships, and private scholarships. The university scholarships are both need-based and academic-based.

Special Opportunities

The Rome Studies Program is required for all students. Third-year architecture students spend the entire academic year in Rome. Additionally, students may choose a concentration in Architectural Practice & Enterprise; Furniture Design; or Preservation & Restoration. There are also minors available in Italian; Sustainability; Energy Studies; Resiliency and Sustainability of Engineering Systems; or Real Estate.

Notable Alumni

Gene Bertoncini, John Burgee, Francis D.K. Ching, Marianne Cusato, Eugenio Rayneri Piedra, and Dan Rockhill

IOWA STATE UNIVERSITY

Address: 715 Bissell Rd, Ames, IA 50011
Website: *https://www.design.iastate.edu/*
Contact: *https://www.design.iastate.edu/college/contact/college-and-departmental-contacts/*
Phone: (515) 294-4111
Email: admissions@iastate.edu

COST OF ATTENDANCE:

In-State Tuition & Fees: $9,634 | **Additional Expenses:** $12,518
Total: $22,152

Out-of-State Tuition & Fees: $25,446 | **Additional Expenses:** $12,518
Total: $37,964

Financial Aid: https://www.financialaid.iastate.edu/

ADDITIONAL INFORMATION:

Available Degree(s)

- Bachelor of Architecture (B.Arch.) - 5-year
- Bachelor of Landscape Architecture (B.L.A.)

Graduate Degree(s)

- Master of Architecture (M.Arch.)
- M.S. Architecture

Portfolio Requirement

There is no portfolio requirement for first-year applicants. After the first year of undergraduate study, a portfolio is required.

Scholarships Offered

First-year undergraduate design students are eligible for the David Stein Memorial Scholarship ($2000), the Chi and Pam Chiu Design Scholarship ($1250), the DAC Scholarship ($1000), and more.

Special Opportunities

Students secure an internship domestically or abroad. These hours go towards the licensure requirement. Class trips are also held, and students travel to urban centers nationwide each semester. Iowa State University also offers an Undeclared Design major for students who would like to explore the various design disciplines before declaring their major.

Notable Alumni

Pamela Abalu, Conde McCullough, and Alyanna Subayno

ILLINOIS

INDIANA

IOWA

KANSAS

MICHIGAN

MINNESOTA

MISSOURI

NEBRASKA

NORTH DAKOTA

OHIO

SOUTH DAKOTA

WISCONSIN

MIDWEST

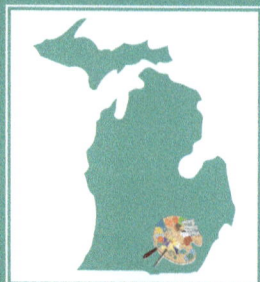

ILLINOIS

INDIANA

IOWA

KANSAS

MICHIGAN

MINNESOTA

MISSOURI

NEBRASKA

NORTH DAKOTA

OHIO

SOUTH DAKOTA

WISCONSIN

UNIVERSITY OF MICHIGAN

Address: 500 S. State St., Ann Arbor, MI 48109
Website: *https://taubmancollege.umich.edu/architecture/degrees/bachelor-science*
Contact: *https://umich.edu/contact/*
Phone: (734) 764-7433
Email: https://admissions.umich.edu/explore-visit/contact-us

COST OF ATTENDANCE:

In-State Tuition & Fees: $15,558 | **Additional Expenses:** $15,498
Total: $31,056

Out-of-State Tuition & Fees: $51,200 | **Additional Expenses:** $15,498
Total: $66,698

Financial Aid: https://finaid.umich.edu/

ADDITIONAL INFORMATION:

Available Degree(s)

- B.S. Architecture

Graduate Degree(s)

- Master of Architecture (M.Arch.)
- Master of Urban Design (M.U.D.)
- M.S. Architecture
- Ph.D. Architecture

Portfolio Requirement

A portfolio is required and must be submitted to SlideRoom. Applicants must include 8-10 works.

Scholarships Offered

University of Michigan offers several scholarships for incoming students. One of them is the Stamps Scholars Program, a prestigious merit-based program that offers the full cost of attendance. The HAIL Scholarship is an invitational award that covers four years of tuition and fees for low-income, high achieving Michigan students. Many scholarships are need-based, although some are merit-based as well.

Special Opportunities

Architecture students at UMich are immersed in analytical and conceptual thinking along with interactive studios and seminars. The design studio is over 32,000 square feet and contains a digital fabrication laboratory. The student to faculty ratio is 12:1 and many students study abroad.

Notable Alumni

James Chaffers, Charles Correa, Daniel L. Dworsky, Karen Fairbanks, Kristina Ford, Robert J. Frasca, Marlene Imirzian, Marcy Kaptur, Peter Kuttner, Peter Lagerwey, Robert C. Metcalf, Jorge Perez, Ralph Rapson, James van Sweden, Tom Tjaarda, Joseph M. Valerio, and Sim Van der Ryn

UNIVERSITY OF MINNESOTA

Address: 330 21st Ave S., Minneapolis, MN 55455
Website: *https://design.umn.edu/academics/programs/about-architecture*
Contact: *http://umn.force.com/admissions/*
Phone: (612) 625-6699
Email: https://admit.umn.edu/register/askaquestion

COST OF ATTENDANCE:

In-State Tuition & Fees: $15,236 | **Additional Expenses:** $16,082
Total: $31,318

Out-of-State Tuition & Fees: $33,534 | **Additional Expenses:** $17,582
Total: $51,116

Financial Aid: https://admissions.tc.umn.edu/costsaid/index.html

ADDITIONAL INFORMATION:

Available Degree(s)

- B.S. Architecture
- Bachelor of Design in Architecture (B.D.A.)

Graduate Degree(s)

- Master of Architecture (M.Arch.)
- Master of Heritage Studies and Public History
- M.S. Architecture, tracks: Sustainable Design; Metropolitan Design; Research Practices
- Ph.D. Design: Architecture

Portfolio Requirement

There is no portfolio requirement.

Scholarships Offered

University of Minnesota offers numerous scholarship opportunities to all students, including in-state and out-of-state students. The University-Wide Academic Scholarships are highly competitive and have varying award amounts. In addition, all international students are automatically considered for the Global Excellence Scholarship ($10,000-$25,000 per year for up to four years).

Special Opportunities

The School of Architecture is located near the bustling metropolitan area of Minneapolis. More than 250 design firms work with the school locally and internationally.

Notable Alumni

Lawrence B. Anderson, George H. Carsley, George Dahl, Matt Dean, Raymond Dehn, Tammy Eagle Bull, Carl Graffunder, Ralph Warner Hammett, Nathan Juran, Kobi Karp, Joel Moss, Charles E. Peterson, John Sheehy, Sarah Susanka, Mark G. Swenson, Lou Waters, Donald Wexler, and Ian Woodner

ILLINOIS

INDIANA

IOWA

KANSAS

MICHIGAN

MINNESOTA

MISSOURI

NEBRASKA

NORTH DAKOTA

OHIO

SOUTH DAKOTA

WISCONSIN

MIDWEST

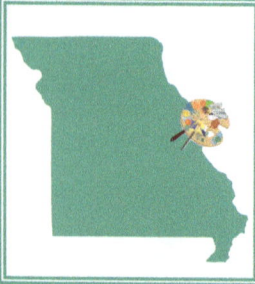

ILLINOIS

INDIANA

IOWA

KANSAS

MICHIGAN

MINNESOTA

MISSOURI

NEBRASKA

NORTH DAKOTA

OHIO

SOUTH DAKOTA

WISCONSIN

WASHINGTON UNIVERSITY IN ST. LOUIS

Address: 1 Brookings Dr., St. Louis, MO 63130
Website: *https://samfoxschool.wustl.edu/academics/college-of-architecture*
Contact: *https://admissions.wustl.edu/contact-us/*
Phone: (314) 935-5858
Email: admissions@wustl.edu

COST OF ATTENDANCE:

Tuition & Fees: $57,750 | **Additional Expenses:** $19,016
Total: $76,766

Financial Aid: https://financialaid.wustl.edu/

ADDITIONAL INFORMATION:

Available degree(s):

- B.A. Architecture
- B.S. Architecture

Graduate Degree(s)

- Master of Architecture (M.Arch.)
- Master of Landscape Architecture (M.L.A.)
- Master of Urban Design (M.U.D.)
- M.S. Advanced Architectural Design
- M.S. Architectural Studies
- Doctor of Sustainable Urbanism (DrSU)

Portfolio Requirement

Portfolios are optional for first-year admission, however they are required for transfers. Submit a 10-20 image portfolio through SlideRoom or have it reviewed in person at a National Portfolio Day or during a scheduled campus visit. Do not include a website link in lieu of submitting a portfolio in SlideRoom.

Scholarships Offered

Students may submit a digital portfolio to be considered for the James W. Fitzgibbon Scholarship in Architecture. WashU offers merit-based and need-based scholarships for students in any major. Some of these institutional scholarships cover the full cost of tuition. They also offer the Signature Scholar Program, which involves individual applications and a weekend program. Partial and full tuition are offered within this scholarship program.

Special Opportunities

Students may study architecture abroad in Spain or Italy. Architecture students also enjoy public lectures, Fox Fridays workshops, and hands-on design studio craft-making. Minors are offered in Architectural History & Theory, Creative Practice for Social Change, Landscape Architecture, or Urban Design.

Notable Alumni

Charles Eames, Hugh Ferriss, Alan Goldberg, Gyo Obata, James F. O'Gorman, and C.P. Wang

CHAPTER 13

REGION THREE

SOUTH

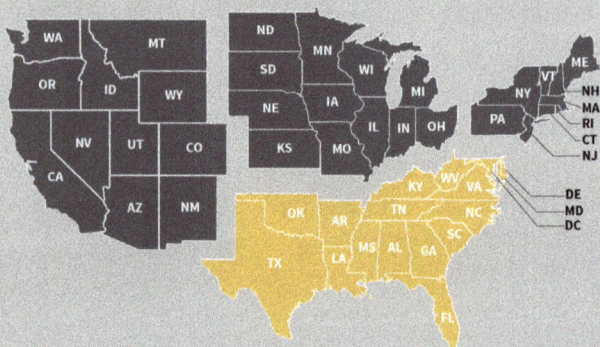

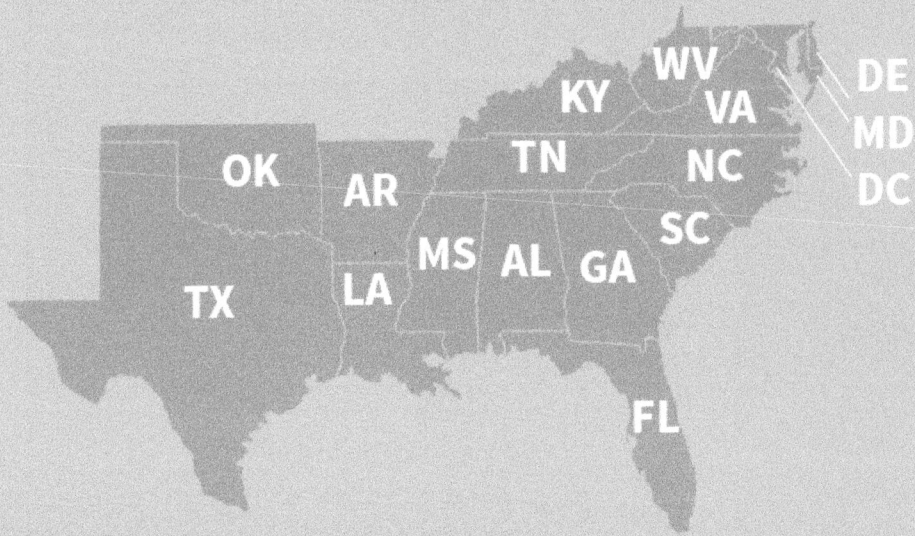

23 Programs | 16 States

1. AL - Auburn University
2. AL - Tuskegee University
3. AR – University of Arkansas
4. DC - Howard University
5. FL - Florida A&M University
6. FL – Florida Atlantic University
7. FL - University of Florida, Gainesville
8. FL - University of Miami
9. GA - Georgia Institute of Technology
10. GA - Savannah College of Art and Design (SCAD)
11. LA - Louisiana State University (LSU)
12. LA - Tulane University
13. NC - North Carolina State University (NC State)
14. NC - University of North Carolina at Charlotte
15. OK - Oklahoma State University
16. OK - University of Oklahoma
17. TN - The University of Tennessee, Knoxville
18. TX - Rice University
19. TX - Texas A&M University
20. TX - University of Houston
21. TX - The University of Texas at Austin (UT Austin)
22. VA - University of Virginia
23. VA - Virginia Polytechnic State University

ARCHITECTURE PROGRAMS

School	Avg. GPA, SAT Evidence-Based Reading Writing (ERW), SAT Math (M), and ACT Composite (C) Early Decision (ED): Yes/No	Admission Statistics	Program(s)	Portfolio Required (req.)
Auburn University 361 Graves Dr, Auburn, AL 36849	GPA: 3.97 SAT (ERW): 590-650 SAT (M): 580-680 ACT (C): 24-30 ED: No	Overall College Admit Rate: 71% Undergrad Enrollment: 24,931 Total Enrollment: 31,526	Bachelor of Architecture (B.Arch.) - 5-year Bachelor of Interior Architecture B.S. Environmental Design Bachelor of Landscape Architecture (B.L.A.) Graduate Degree(s): Master of Building Construction Master of Landscape Architecture (M.L.A.) Master of Industrial Design M.S. Architecture Degrees Awarded in the Program(s): 115	Portfolio not req.

School	Avg. GPA, SAT Evidence-Based Reading Writing (ERW), SAT Math (M), and ACT Composite (C) Early Decision (ED): Yes/No	Admission Statistics	Program(s)	Portfolio Required (req.)
Tuskegee University 1200 W. Montgomery Rd., Tuskegee, AL 36088	GPA: 3 SAT (ERW): 450-525 SAT (M): 410-520 ACT (C): 18-24 ED: No	Overall College Admit Rate: 61% Undergrad Enrollment: 2,280 Total Enrollment: 2,747	B.Arch Bachelor of Architecture (B.Arch) Degrees Awarded in the Program(s): 4	Portfolio not req.
University of Arkansas 120 Vol Walker Hall, Fayetteville, AR 72701	GPA: 3.75 SAT (ERW): 550-640 SAT (M): 540-640 ACT (C): 23-29 ED: No	Overall College Admit Rate: 78% Undergrad Enrollment: 22,825 Total Enrollment: 27,562	Bachelor of Architecture (B.Arch.) - 5-year B.S. Architectural Studies (B.S.A.S.) Bachelor of Interior Design (B.I.D.) Bachelor of Landscape Architecture (B.L.A.) B.S. Landscape Architectural Studies Graduate Degree(s): Master of Design Studies Degrees Awarded in the Program(s): 60	Portfolio not req.

SOUTH

ARCHITECTURE PROGRAMS

School	Avg. GPA, SAT Evidence-Based Reading Writing (ERW), SAT Math (M), and ACT Composite (C) Early Decision (ED): Yes/No	Admission Statistics	Program(s)	Portfolio Required (req.)
Howard University 2366 Sixth Street, NW Washington, DC 20059	GPA: 3.55 SAT (ERW): 580-640 SAT (M): 550-620 ACT (C): 22-26 ED: Yes	Overall College Admit Rate: 39% Undergrad Enrollment: 7,857 Total Enrollment: 10,859	Master of Architecture (M.Arch.) - 5-year (incorporating the bachelor's degree) Degrees Awarded in the Program(s): 7	Portfolio req.
Florida A&M University 1938 S. Martin Luther King Jr. Blvd., Walter L. Smith Architecture Building, Tallahassee, FL 32307	GPA: 3.5 SAT (ERW): 520-590 SAT (M): 510-560 ACT (C): 20-24 ED: No	Overall College Admit Rate: 33% Undergrad Enrollment: 7,402 Total Enrollment: 9,184	Bachelor of Architecture (B.Arch.) - 5-year B.S. Architectural Studies Graduate Degree(s): Master of Architecture (M.Arch.) M.S. Architecture Degrees Awarded in the Program(s): 37	Portfolio not req.
Florida Atlantic University 111 East Las Olas Boulevard, Fort Lauderdale, FL 33301	GPA: 3.74 SAT (ERW): 540-620 SAT (M): 520-600 ACT (C): 21-26 ED: No	Overall College Admit Rate: 75% Undergrad Enrollment: 25,457 Total Enrollment: 30,805	Bachelor of Architecture (B.Arch.) - 5-year B.Arch./Master of Urban and Regional Planning (M.U.R.P.) Degrees Awarded in the Program(s): 66	Portfolio not req.

ARCHITECTURE PROGRAMS

School	Avg. GPA, SAT Evidence-Based Reading Writing (ERW), SAT Math (M), and ACT Composite (C) Early Decision (ED): Yes/No	Admission Statistics	Program(s)	Portfolio Required (req.)
University of Florida, Gainesville University of Florida, Gainesville, FL 32611	GPA: 3.88 SAT (ERW): 650-720 SAT (M): 640-740 ACT (C): 29-33 ED: No	Overall College Admit Rate: 31% Undergrad Enrollment: 34,931 Total Enrollment: 53,372	Bachelor of Design in Architecture (B.Des. Arch.) Bachelor of Landscape Architecture (B.L.A.) Degrees Awarded in the Program(s): 98	Portfolio not req.

SOUTH

ARCHITECTURE PROGRAMS

School	Avg. GPA, SAT Evidence-Based Reading Writing (ERW), SAT Math (M), and ACT Composite (C) Early Decision (ED): Yes/No	Admission Statistics	Program(s)	Portfolio Required (req.)
University of Miami 1223 Dickinson Drive, Coral Gables, FL 33146	GPA: 3.6 SAT (ERW): 620-700 SAT (M): 630-720 ACT (C): 28-32 ED: Yes	Overall College Admit Rate: 33% Undergrad Enrollment: 11,334 Total Enrollment: 17,809	Bachelor of Architecture (B.Arch.) - 5-year B.S. Architectural Engineering/M. Arch. Graduate Degree(s): Master of Architecture (M.Arch.) M.S. Architecture Master of Urban Design (M.U.D.) Master of Real Estate Development and Urbanism (M.R.E.D.+U) Master of Construction Management (M.C.M.) Degrees Awarded in the Program(s): 43	Portfolio optional
Georgia Institute of Technology Georgia Institute of Technology, North Ave NW, Atlanta, GA 30332	GPA: 4.09 SAT (ERW): 670-740 SAT (M): 700-790 ACT (C): 31-35 ED: No	Overall College Admit Rate: 21% Undergrad Enrollment: 16,561 Total Enrollment: 39,771	Bachelor of Architecture (B.Arch.) - 5-year Degrees Awarded in the Program(s): 32	Portfolio optional

ARCHITECTURE PROGRAMS

School	Avg. GPA, SAT Evidence-Based Reading Writing (ERW), SAT Math (M), and ACT Composite (C) Early Decision (ED): Yes/No	Admission Statistics	Program(s)	Portfolio Required (req.)
Savannah College of Art and Design (SCAD) 342 Bull St., Savannah, GA 31401	GPA: 3.6 SAT (ERW): 540-640 SAT (M): 500-600 ACT (C): 20-27 ED: No	Overall College Admit Rate: 78% Undergrad Enrollment: 11,679 Total Enrollment: 14,265	BFA Architecture Graduate Degree(s): Master of Architecture (M.Arch.) Degrees Awarded in the Program(s): 67	Portfolio optional
Louisiana State University (LSU) 102 Design Building, Baton Rouge, LA 70803	GPA: 3.45 SAT (ERW): 550-660 SAT (M): 540-640 ACT (C): 23-28 ED: No	Overall College Admit Rate: 73% Undergrad Enrollment: 27,825 Total Enrollment: 34,285	Bachelor of Architecture (B.Arch.) Graduate Degree(s): Master of Architecture (M.Arch.) Degrees Awarded in the Program(s): 75	Portfolio not req.
Tulane University 6823 St. Charles Ave., New Orleans, LA 70118	GPA: 3.64 SAT (ERW): 680-740 SAT (M): 680-770 ACT (C): 30-33 ED: Yes	Overall College Admit Rate: 10% Undergrad Enrollment: 7,780 Total Enrollment: 13,127	B.S. Architecture Bachelor of Architecture (B.Arch.) Degrees Awarded in the Program(s): 43	Portfolio optional

SOUTH

ARCHITECTURE PROGRAMS

School	Avg. GPA, SAT Evidence-Based Reading Writing (ERW), SAT Math (M), and ACT Composite (C) Early Decision (ED): Yes/No	Admission Statistics	Program(s)	Portfolio Required (req.)
North Carolina State University (NC State) 50 Pullen Road, Raleigh, NC 27695	GPA: 3.8 SAT (ERW): 620-690 SAT (M): 630-730 ACT (C): 27-32 ED: No	Overall College Admit Rate: 46% Undergrad Enrollment: 26,150 Total Enrollment: 36,042	Bachelor of Environmental Design (B.E.D.A.) Bachelor of Architecture (B.Arch.) - 1-year* Graduate Degree(s): Master of Architecture (M.Arch.) Master of Advanced Architectural Studies (M.A.A.S.) Degrees Awarded in the Program(s): 60	Portfolio req.
University of North Carolina at Charlotte 9201 University City Boulevard, Charlotte, NC 28223	GPA: 3.92 SAT (ERW): 560-640 SAT (M): 560-640 ACT (C): 22-27 ED: No	Overall College Admit Rate: 80% Undergrad Enrollment: 24,175 Total Enrollment: 30,146	B.A. Architecture Degrees Awarded in the Program(s): 61	Portfolio req.

School	Avg. GPA, SAT Evidence-Based Reading Writing (ERW), SAT Math (M), and ACT Composite (C) Early Decision (ED): Yes/No	Admission Statistics	Program(s)	Portfolio Required (req.)
Oklahoma State University Oklahoma State University, Stillwater, OK 74078	GPA: 3.59 SAT (ERW): 540-640 SAT (M): 520-640 ACT (C): 22-28 ED: No	Overall College Admit Rate: 67% Undergrad Enrollment: 20,323 Total Enrollment: 24,535	Bachelor of Architecture (B.Arch.) - 5-year Bachelor of Architectural Engineering - 5-year Degrees Awarded in the Program(s): 43	Portfolio not req.

SOUTH

ARCHITECTURE PROGRAMS

School	Avg. GPA, SAT Evidence-Based Reading Writing (ERW), SAT Math (M), and ACT Composite (C) Early Decision (ED): Yes/No	Admission Statistics	Program(s)	Portfolio Required (req.)
University of Oklahoma 830 Van Vleet Oval, Norman, OK 73019	GPA: 3.63 SAT (ERW): 560-650 SAT (M): 540-650 ACT (C): 23-29 ED: No	Overall College Admit Rate: 83% Undergrad Enrollment: 21,383 Total Enrollment: 27,772	Bachelor of Architecture (B.Arch.) - 5-year Bachelor of Construction Science B.S. Environmental Design B.S. Architectural Studies (B.S.A.S.) Bachelor of Interior Design Graduate Degree(s): Master of Architecture (M.Arch.) Master of Landscape Architectural Studies Master of Urban Design M.S. Planning, Design, and Construction Ph.D. Planning, Design, and Construction Degrees Awarded in the Program(s): 15	Portfolio not req.

School	Avg. GPA, SAT Evidence-Based Reading Writing (ERW), SAT Math (M), and ACT Composite (C) Early Decision (ED): Yes/No	Admission Statistics	Program(s)	Portfolio Required (req.)
The University of Tennessee, Knoxville 1715 Volunteer Blvd, Knoxville, TN 37996	GPA: 3.96 SAT (ERW): 580-650 SAT (M): 560-653 ACT (C): 25-31 ED: No	Overall College Admit Rate: 78% Undergrad Enrollment: 24,254 Total Enrollment: 30,559	Bachelor of Architecture (B.Arch.) - 5-year B.S. Interior Architecture Graduate Degree(s): Master of Architecture (M.Arch.) Master of Landscape Architecture (M.L.A.) Degrees Awarded in the Program(s): 90	Portfolio optional
Rice University 6100 Main Street, Houston, TX 77005	GPA: N/A SAT (ERW): 710-770 SAT (M): 750-800 ACT (C): 34-36 ED: Yes	Overall College Admit Rate: 11% Undergrad Enrollment: 4,076 Total Enrollment: 7,643	B.A. Architecture/ Bachelor of Architecture (B.Arch.) - 6-year dual degree Degrees Awarded in the Program(s): 39	Portfolio req.

SOUTH

ARCHITECTURE PROGRAMS

School	Avg. GPA, SAT Evidence-Based Reading Writing (ERW), SAT Math (M), and ACT Composite (C) / Early Decision (ED): Yes/No	Admission Statistics	Program(s)	Portfolio Required (req.)
Texas A&M University 400 Bizzell St, College Station, TX 77843	GPA: N/A SAT (ERW): 580-680 SAT (M): 580-800 ACT (C): 26-32 ED: No	Overall College Admit Rate: 63% Undergrad Enrollment: 55,568 Total Enrollment: 70,418	Bachelor of Landscape Architecture (B.L.A.) B.S. Environmental Design B.S. Construction Science B.S. Urban and Regional Planning B.S. Visualization Graduate Degree(s): Master of Architecture (M.Arch.) M.S. Architecture M.S. Land & Property Development M.S. Landscape Architecture M.S. Urban Planning Ph.D. Architecture Ph.D. Construction Science Ph.D. Urban and Regional Sciences Degrees Awarded in the Program(s): 198	Portfolio not req.

School	Avg. GPA, SAT Evidence-Based Reading Writing (ERW), SAT Math (M), and ACT Composite (C) Early Decision (ED): Yes/No	Admission Statistics	Program(s)	Portfolio Required (req.)
University of Houston 4200 Elgin Street, Room 122, Houston, TX 77204	GPA: 3.73 SAT (ERW): 560-650 SAT (M): 560-660 ACT (C): 22-28 ED: No	Overall College Admit Rate: 63% Undergrad Enrollment: 39,165 Total Enrollment: 47,090	Bachelor of Architecture (B.Arch.) - 5-year B.S. Interior Architecture B.S. Industrial Design B.S. Environmental Design Graduate Degree(s): Master of Architecture (M.Arch.) M.A. Architectural Studies M.S. Architecture M.S. Industrial Design Degrees Awarded in the Program(s): 90	Portfolio req.

SOUTH

ARCHITECTURE PROGRAMS

School	Avg. GPA, SAT Evidence-Based Reading Writing (ERW), SAT Math (M), and ACT Composite (C) Early Decision (ED): Yes/No	Admission Statistics	Program(s)	Portfolio Required (req.)
The University of Texas at Austin (UT Austin) 310 Inner Campus Drive, Austin, TX 78712	GPA: N/A SAT (ERW): 610-720 SAT (M): 600-750 ACT (C): 26-33 ED: No	Overall College Admit Rate: 32% Undergrad Enrollment: 40,048 Total Enrollment: 50,476	Bachelor of Architecture (B.Arch.) - 5-year B.S. Architectural Studies (B.S.A.S.) B.S. Interior Design B.S. Architectural Engineering Graduate Degree(s): Master of Architecture (M.Arch.) Master of Interior Design Degrees Awarded in the Program(s): 45	Portfolio not req.
University of Virginia University of Virginia, Charlottesville, VA 22904	GPA: 4.31 SAT (ERW): 660-740 SAT (M): 660-770 ACT (C): 30-34 ED: Yes	Overall College Admit Rate: 23% Undergrad Enrollment: 17,310 Total Enrollment: 25,628	B.S. Architecture Degrees Awarded in the Program(s): 76	Portfolio not req.

School	Avg. GPA, SAT Evidence-Based Reading Writing (ERW), SAT Math (M), and ACT Composite (C) Early Decision (ED): Yes/No	Admission Statistics	Program(s)	Portfolio Required (req.)
Virginia Polytechnic State University 1325 Perry Street, Blacksburg, VA 24061	GPA: 3.96 SAT (ERW): 590-680 SAT (M): 580-690 ACT (C): 25-31 ED: Yes	Overall College Admit Rate: 66% Undergrad Enrollment: 30,020 Total Enrollment: 37,024	Bachelor of Architecture (B.Arch.) - 5-year B.S. Industrial Design B.S. Interior Design Bachelor of Landscape Architecture (B.L.A.) Graduate Degree(s): Master of Architecture (M.Arch.) Master of Landscape Architecture (M.L.A.) M.S. Architecture, concentrations: Building Science; Urban Design Degrees Awarded in the Program(s): 123	Portfolio not req.

SOUTH

ALABAMA

ARKANSAS

DELAWARE

DISTRICT OF
COLUMBIA

FLORIDA

GEORGIA

KENTUCKY

LOUISIANA

MARYLAND

MISSISSIPPI

NORTH CAROLINA

OKLAHOMA

SOUTH CAROLINA

TENNESSEE

TEXAS

VIRGINIA

WEST VIRGINIA

AUBURN UNIVERSITY

Address: 361 Graves Dr, Auburn, AL 36849
Website: *https://cadc.auburn.edu/*
Contact: *https://cadc.auburn.edu/contact/*
Phone: (334) 844-4516
Email: aucadc@auburn.edu

COST OF ATTENDANCE:

In-State Tuition & Fees: $11,796 | **Additional Expenses:** $21,648
Total: $33,444

Out-of-State Tuition & Fees: $31,956 | **Additional Expenses:** $21,648
Total: $53,604

Financial Aid: http://www.auburn.edu/administration/business-finance/finaid/

ADDITIONAL INFORMATION:

Available Degree(s)

- Bachelor of Architecture (B.Arch.) - 5-year
- Bachelor of Interior Architecture
- B.S. Environmental Design
- Bachelor of Landscape Architecture (B.L.A.)

Graduate Degree(s)

- Master of Building Construction
- Master of Landscape Architecture (M.L.A.)
- Master of Industrial Design
- M.S. Architecture

Portfolio Requirement

Portfolios are not required nor accepted.

Scholarships Offered

Merit-based and need-based aid are available. Non-resident merit scholarships are up to $15,000 and resident merit scholarships go up to $8,000. CADC awards approximately $200,000 in scholarships each year. Submission of the FAFSA is not required, though it is recommended for major-specific scholarships.

Special Opportunities

Auburn engages students in master planning, community development, and urban design projects through their Urban Studio of downtown Birmingham. Students' international design projects have been engaged in a half dozen countries. With the title "Educating Citizen Architects", Auburn established its Rural Studio, an off-campus design-build program to create sustainable, scalable, and affordable rural living and systems for underserved areas.

Notable Alumni

Marlon Blackwell, Rob Burton, Jim Gorrie, Harold Goyette, Michael Harris, Tom Hardy, Samuel Mockbee, and Paul Rudolph

TUSKEGEE UNIVERSITY

Address: 1200 W. Montgomery Rd., Tuskegee, AL 36088
Website: *https://www.tuskegee.edu/programs-courses/colleges-schools/tsacs*
Contact: *https://www.tuskegee.edu/programs-courses/colleges-schools/tsacs/program-overview#*
Phone: (334) 727-8011
Email: tsacs@tuskegee.edu

COST OF ATTENDANCE:

Tuition & Fees: $22,614 | **Additional Expenses:** $10,746
Total: $33,360

Financial Aid: https://www.tuskegee.edu/admissions-aid/financial-aid

ADDITIONAL INFORMATION:

Available Degree(s)

- Bachelor of Architecture (B.Arch.) - 5-year

Portfolio Requirement

Portfolios are not required for first-year applicants. Portfolios are only required for the professional program in the third year. The first two years of study are pre-professional.

Scholarships Offered

Merit scholarships available with various award amounts. The highest merit scholarship is the Distinguished Presidential scholarship covers full tuition, room/board, fees, and $800 for books. The lower end of the merit scholarship awards is still high, with an award of $8,000.

Special Opportunities

Architecture majors may be interested in pursuing a minor in Historic Preservation, the Built Environment, or Construction Science.

Notable Alumni

John A. Lankford

ALABAMA
ARKANSAS
DELAWARE
DISTRICT OF COLUMBIA
FLORIDA
GEORGIA
KENTUCKY
LOUISIANA
MARYLAND
MISSISSIPPI
NORTH CAROLINA
OKLAHOMA
SOUTH CAROLINA
TENNESSEE
TEXAS
VIRGINIA
WEST VIRGINIA

SOUTH

UNIVERSITY OF ARKANSAS

Address: 120 Vol Walker Hall, Fayetteville, AR 72701
Website: *https://fayjones.uark.edu/*
Contact: *https://fayjones.uark.edu/about/contact-and-visit/index.php*
Phone: (479) 575-4945
Email: fjsoa@uark.edu

COST OF ATTENDANCE:

In-State Tuition & Fees: $9,384 | **Additional Expenses:** $16,760
Total: $26,144

Out-of-State Tuition & Fees: $25,872 | **Additional Expenses:** $16,760
Total: $42,632

Financial Aid: https://finaid.uark.edu/financial_aid_information/index.php

ADDITIONAL INFORMATION:

Available Degree(s)

- Bachelor of Architecture (B.Arch.) - 5-year
- B.S. Architectural Studies (B.S.A.S.)
- Bachelor of Interior Design (B.I.D.)
- Bachelor of Landscape Architecture (B.L.A.)
- B.S. Landscape Architectural Studies

Graduate Degree(s)

- Master of Design Studies

Portfolio Requirement

Portfolios are not required for applicants. However, there are specific requirements for applicants to follow. There are two tracks of study for entering freshmen: the fall/spring studio students or the summer/summer studio students. Students may gain admission to the Fall/Spring Studio if they meet the following requirements:

- ACT of 25+
- 3.5+ high school GPA
- College preparatory coursework that includes physics and an upper-level math

The Fall/Spring Studio track is limited to 120 students and priority is given to students who indicate architecture or architectural studies as their intended major by November 15th.

Scholarships Offered

Fay Jones School of Architecture and Design offers numerous need-based and merit-based scholarships. There are 34 scholarships for architecture students at varying points of their undergraduate studies. These awards are based on financial need and merit.

Special Opportunities

Architecture students may be interested in minoring in the following: History of Architecture and Design, Interior Design, Planning, and Sustainability.

Notable Alumni

E. Fay Jones and Edward Durell Stone

ALABAMA
ARKANSAS
DELAWARE
DISTRICT OF COLUMBIA
FLORIDA
GEORGIA
KENTUCKY
LOUISIANA
MARYLAND
MISSISSIPPI
NORTH CAROLINA
OKLAHOMA
SOUTH CAROLINA
TENNESSEE
TEXAS
VIRGINIA
WEST VIRGINIA

164

HOWARD UNIVERSITY

Address: 2366 Sixth Street, NW Washington, DC 20059
Website: *http://www.arch.cea.howard.edu/*
Contact: *https://www2.howard.edu/contact*
Phone: (202) 806-7424
Email: admission@howard.edu

COST OF ATTENDANCE:

Tuition & Fees: $28,916 | **Additional Expenses:** $19,198
Total: $48,114

Financial Aid: http://www.arch.cea.howard.edu/financial-aid

ADDITIONAL INFORMATION:

Available Degree(s)

- Master of Architecture (M.Arch.) - 5-year (incorporating the bachelor's degree)

Portfolio Requirement

A portfolio is required. It must include 1-3 examples of creative work in graphic, written, or audiovisual form. Submission is via email.

Scholarships Offered

Howard University offers freshman scholarships (HUFS) such as the HU Presidential Scholarship, HU Founders Scholarship, etc. Award amounts vary and are not listed.

Special Opportunities

This program is unique in that high school seniors apply directly to the 5-year architecture program that leads to a Master of Architecture (M.Arch.). The bachelor's degree is incorporated into the M.Arch. This new curriculum was introduced in Fall 2018.

Notable Alumni

Louis Arnett Stuart Bellinger and Harry G. Robinson III

ALABAMA

ARKANSAS

DELAWARE

DISTRICT OF COLUMBIA

FLORIDA

GEORGIA

KENTUCKY

LOUISIANA

MARYLAND

MISSISSIPPI

NORTH CAROLINA

OKLAHOMA

SOUTH CAROLINA

TENNESSEE

TEXAS

VIRGINIA

WEST VIRGINIA

SOUTH

ALABAMA

ARKANSAS

DELAWARE

DISTRICT OF
COLUMBIA

FLORIDA

GEORGIA

KENTUCKY

LOUISIANA

MARYLAND

MISSISSIPPI

NORTH CAROLINA

OKLAHOMA

SOUTH CAROLINA

TENNESSEE

TEXAS

VIRGINIA

WEST VIRGINIA

FLORIDA A&M UNIVERSITY

Address: 1938 S. Martin Luther King Jr. Blvd., Walter L. Smith Architecture Building, Tallahassee, FL 32307
Website: *https://saet.famu.edu/index.php*
Contact: *https://admissions.famu.edu/talk-to-admissions.php*
Phone: (850) 599-3244
Email: ugrdadmissions@famu.edu

COST OF ATTENDANCE:

In-State Tuition & Fees: $4,694 | **Additional Expenses:** $18,738
Total: $23,432

Out-of-State Tuition & Fees: $17,730 | **Additional Expenses:** $17,648
Total: $35,378

Financial Aid: http://www.famu.edu/index.cfm?FinancialAid

ADDITIONAL INFORMATION:

Available Degree(s)

- Bachelor of Architecture (B.Arch.) - 5-year
- B.S. Architectural Studies

Graduate Degree(s)

- Master of Architecture (M.Arch.)
- M.S. Architecture

Portfolio Requirement

Portfolios are not required for incoming freshmen applicants. A portfolio review happens after the first year.

Scholarships Offered

The School of Architecture and Engineering Technology offers various scholarships from architectural firms, for students from Caribbean countries, and for African American students.

Special Opportunities

The School of Architecture and Engineering Technology is housed in two buildings: the Walter L. Smith Architecture Building, and the Benjamin Banneker complex. The Walter L. Smith Architecture Building spans 100,000 square feet and includes classrooms, technology labs, design studios, a model shop, and a building construction lab. The Benjamin Banneker complex includes specialized laboratory testing and computer labs.

Notable Alumni

Dario McPhee, Ana Pichardo, Jomarie Santiago, and Maxcell Spriggs

FLORIDA ATLANTIC UNIVERSITY

Address: 111 East Las Olas Boulevard, Fort Lauderdale, FL 33301
Website: *http://cdsi.fau.edu/soa/*
Contact: *http://cdsi.fau.edu/soa/about/contacts/*
Phone: (954) 762-5654
Email: admissions@fau.edu

COST OF ATTENDANCE:

In-State Tuition & Fees: $5,642 | **Additional Expenses:** $19,974
Total: $25,616

Out-of-State Tuition & Fees: $19,642 | **Additional Expenses:** $19,974
Total: $39,616

Financial Aid: http://www.fau.edu/finaid/

ADDITIONAL INFORMATION:

Available Degree(s)

- Bachelor of Architecture (B.Arch.) - 5-year
- B.Arch./Master of Urban and Regional Planning (M.U.R.P.)

Portfolio Requirement

First-year applicants are not required to submit a portfolio. Students are automatically considered for entry into the lower division architecture program. Priority deadline is January 31. There is a second admission review process for entry into the upper division architecture program. This second process requires a portfolio.

Scholarships Offered

Milton & Gladys Meisner Scholarship Fund is available to architecture students in their third or fourth years with financial need. In addition, the Lawrence P. and Dorothy E. DeLisle Memorial Scholarship is available to architecture students with a 3.0+ GPA and financial need. Other merit-based and need-based scholarships are also available.

Special Opportunities

The lower division architecture program is on the Boca Raton Campus. The upper division program is on the Fort Lauderdale campus. Students have the option to study abroad, in locations such as Germany (Dessau, Berlin, and Rosenheim), Thailand, and Italy.

In addition, FAU offers the Architecture Summer Institute for High School Students. This is a two-week architecture intensive program to high school students at the Boca Raton campus. Rising sophomores, juniors, and seniors in high school, recent high school graduates, and students in their first two years of college are welcome to apply. Furthermore, current FAU architecture students apply to be a mentor for this program.

Notable Alumni

Mirelys Calise, Emma Chen, Todd Evans, Randy Goin, Jr., Leigh McFarland, Paula Jarrett Nasta, Tabitha Ponte, and Don Pruett

ALABAMA
ARKANSAS
DELAWARE
DISTRICT OF COLUMBIA
FLORIDA
GEORGIA
KENTUCKY
LOUISIANA
MARYLAND
MISSISSIPPI
NORTH CAROLINA
OKLAHOMA
SOUTH CAROLINA
TENNESSEE
TEXAS
VIRGINIA
WEST VIRGINIA

SOUTH

ALABAMA

ARKANSAS

DELAWARE

DISTRICT OF
COLUMBIA

FLORIDA

GEORGIA

KENTUCKY

LOUISIANA

MARYLAND

MISSISSIPPI

NORTH CAROLINA

OKLAHOMA

SOUTH CAROLINA

TENNESSEE

TEXAS

VIRGINIA

WEST VIRGINIA

UNIVERSITY OF FLORIDA, GAINESVILLE

Address: University of Florida, Gainesville, FL 32611
Website: *https://dcp.ufl.edu/architecture/bachelor-of-design/overview/*
Contact: *https://admissions.ufl.edu/contacts*
Phone: (352) 392-1365
Email: freshman@ufl.edu

COST OF ATTENDANCE:

In-State Tuition & Fees: $6,380 | **Additional Expenses:** $15,050
Total: $21,430

Out-of-State Tuition & Fees: $28,658 | **Additional Expenses:** $15,050
Total: $43,708

Financial Aid: http://www.fau.edu/finaid/

ADDITIONAL INFORMATION:

Available Degree(s)

- Bachelor of Design in Architecture (B.Des. Arch.)

Portfolio Requirement

There is no portfolio requirement for incoming freshmen.

Scholarships Offered

University of Florida, Gainesville offers numerous merit-based and need-based scholarships. Presidential Scholarships range from $5,000-$10,000 per year. Furthermore, they offer a limited number of out-of-state tuition waivers.

Special Opportunities

The College of Design Construction and Planning is one of only six colleges in the nation that combine all design and construction disciplines. Architecture students gain an interdisciplinary learning experience.

Notable Alumni

Alberto Alfonso, Carlos J. Alfonso, Alex Anmahian, Stephen Francis Jones, Beatriz del Cueto Lopez, Gene Leedy, Alfred Browning Parker, William Rupp, Lawrence Scarpa, Max Strang, and Andrew Weaver

UNIVERSITY OF MIAMI

Address: 1223 Dickinson Drive, Coral Gables, FL 33146
Website: https://www.arc.miami.edu/
Contact: https://www.arc.miami.edu/about-umsoa/contact-us-and-directions/index.html
Phone: (305) 284 3731
Email: admission@miami.edu

COST OF ATTENDANCE:

Tuition & Fees: $53,682 | **Additional Expenses:** $20,030
Total: $73,712

Financial Aid: https://finaid.miami.edu/index.html

ADDITIONAL INFORMATION:

Available Degree(s)

- Bachelor of Architecture (B.Arch.) - 5-year
- B.S. Architectural Engineering/M.Arch.

Graduate Degree(s)

- Master of Architecture (M.Arch.)
- M.S. Architecture
- Master of Urban Design (M.U.D.)
- Master of Real Estate Development and Urbanism (M.R.E.D.+U)
- Master of Construction Management (M.C.M.)

Portfolio Requirement

Portfolios are not required. However, architecture applicants are highly encouraged to submit one. Students may choose to submit a portfolio in place of an SAT/ACT score. Portfolios are used to evaluate for talent-based scholarships. Submit via the UMiami website.

Scholarships Offered

The most prestigious merit award at UM is the Stamps Scholarship. This scholarship covers the student's full cost of attendance for four years of study, including a laptop allowance and access to a $12,000 enrichment fund that may be used towards educational purposes. Other UM scholarships also cover the full cost of tuition or cost of attendance for all four years. These are all based on merit and/or financial need.

Special Opportunities

Students have the option to take coursework in Rome, Italy. The Rome Program is sponsored by the University of Miami. Undergraduate students, graduate students, faculty, and professionals all take part in this program abroad. Students are accepted into this study abroad opportunity if they meet certain criteria such as GPA, portfolio, and an essay of intention.

The University of Miami offers the D.Arch./MBA, where students earn both degrees simultaneously in six years. Students take Saturday graduate-level M.B.A. coursework during their fourth year.

Notable Alumni

Jaime Correa, Rodolphe el-Khoury, Marion Manley, Elizabeth Plater-Zyberk, and John Llewellyn Skinner

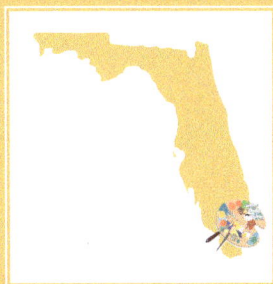

ALABAMA

ARKANSAS

DELAWARE

DISTRICT OF COLUMBIA

FLORIDA

GEORGIA

KENTUCKY

LOUISIANA

MARYLAND

MISSISSIPPI

NORTH CAROLINA

OKLAHOMA

SOUTH CAROLINA

TENNESSEE

TEXAS

VIRGINIA

WEST VIRGINIA

SOUTH

GEORGIA INSTITUTE OF TECHNOLOGY

Address: Georgia Institute of Technology, North Ave NW, Atlanta, GA 30332
Website: *https://arch.gatech.edu/bachelor-science-architecture*
Contact: *https://admission.gatech.edu/contact*
Phone: (404) 894-4154
Email: admission@gatech.edu

COST OF ATTENDANCE:

In-State Tuition & Fees: $12,858 | **Additional Expenses:** $16,640
Total: $29,498

Out-of-State Tuition & Fees: $33,970 | **Additional Expenses:** $16,640
Total: $50,610

Financial Aid: https://finaid.gatech.edu/costs/cost-of-attendance

ADDITIONAL INFORMATION:

Available Degree(s)

- Bachelor of Architecture (B.Arch.) - 5-year

Portfolio Requirement

Although the School of Architecture and Industrial Design do not require portfolios, students are invited to submit pieces to provide insight into visual training, qualifications, and experience. For SOA and SID, applicants will be given a link after Common App submission on your GT status page. Submit no more than 10 high-quality images (original ideas rather than reproductions showing skill and craft in life drawing, painting, design, sculpture, or other media). Architectural drawings are not necessary.

Scholarships Offered

Federal, state, merit aid, and work-study are available.

Special Opportunities

Georgia Tech hosts a prospective "Focus on Design Day". GT has research specializations in Architecture, Culture, & Behavior; Building Design Technology; Design Computation; History, Theory, & Criticism; and Urbanism. The School of Architecture Research Labs includes Flourishing Communities, High-Performance Building, Shape Computation, Spatial Futures. The College of Design has the Digital Building Lab and SimTigrate Design Lab.

Notable Alumni

Cecil Alexander, Michael Arad, Bill Finch, George T. Heery, Jan Lorenc, John C. Portman, Jr., L.W. "Chip" Robert, Jr., and Hugh Stubbins

ALABAMA

ARKANSAS

DELAWARE

DISTRICT OF COLUMBIA

FLORIDA

GEORGIA

KENTUCKY

LOUISIANA

MARYLAND

MISSISSIPPI

NORTH CAROLINA

OKLAHOMA

SOUTH CAROLINA

TENNESSEE

TEXAS

VIRGINIA

WEST VIRGINIA

SAVANNAH COLLEGE OF ART & DESIGN (SCAD)

Address: 342 Bull St., Savannah, GA 31401
Website: *https://www.scad.edu/academics/programs/architecture*
Contact: *https://www.scad.edu/about/contact*
Phone: (912) 525-5100
Email: contact@scad.edu
Other locations: Atlanta, GA

COST OF ATTENDANCE:

Tuition & Fees: $38,340 | **Additional Expenses:** $15,269
Total: $53,609

Financial Aid: https://www.scad.edu/admission/financial-aid-and-scholarships

ADDITIONAL INFORMATION:

Available degree(s):

- B.F.A. Architecture

Graduate Degree(s)

- Master of Architecture (M.Arch.)

Portfolio Requirement

A portfolio and résumé/list of achievements are optional, but they are required for scholarship consideration. Submit through SlideRoom. All work must be original in fabrication and concept.

Scholarships Offered

All applicants including international students are eligible for merit-scholarships. The May and Paul Poetter Scholarship awards full tuition and is based on academic achievement. The Frances Larkin McCommon Scholarship awards full tuition and is based on artistic achievement. SCAD also offers SCAD academic scholarships ($1,500-$12,000). Among grants, the SCAD Athletic Grant awards $2,000-$12,000.

Special Opportunities

SCAD offers dozens of minors and certificates (advertising, animation, costume, drawing, fashion, fragrance, game UX, illustration for entertainment, interactive design, jewelry, mobile design, package design, photography, printmaking, sculpture, sequential art, storyboarding, themed entertainment, user experience, visual effects, voice, writing).

Notable Alumni

Barrera Castaneda

ALABAMA
ARKANSAS
DELAWARE
DISTRICT OF COLUMBIA
FLORIDA
GEORGIA
KENTUCKY
LOUISIANA
MARYLAND
MISSISSIPPI
NORTH CAROLINA
OKLAHOMA
SOUTH CAROLINA
TENNESSEE
TEXAS
VIRGINIA
WEST VIRGINIA

SOUTH

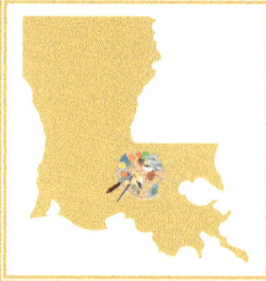

ALABAMA

ARKANSAS

DELAWARE

DISTRICT OF
COLUMBIA

FLORIDA

GEORGIA

KENTUCKY

LOUISIANA

MARYLAND

MISSISSIPPI

NORTH CAROLINA

OKLAHOMA

SOUTH CAROLINA

TENNESSEE

TEXAS

VIRGINIA

WEST VIRGINIA

LOUISIANA STATE UNIVERSITY (LSU)

Address: 102 Design Building, Baton Rouge, LA 70803
Website: *https://design.lsu.edu/*
Contact: *https://lsu.edu/about/requestinfo.php*
Phone: (225) 578-5400
Email: adsn@lsu.edu

COST OF ATTENDANCE:

In-State Tuition & Fees: $11,962 | **Additional Expenses:** $23,088
Total: $35,050

Out-of-State Tuition & Fees: $28,639 | **Additional Expenses:** $23,088
Total: $51,727

Financial Aid: https://www.lsu.edu/financialaid/index.php

ADDITIONAL INFORMATION:

Available Degree(s)

- Bachelor of Architecture (B.Arch.) - 5-year

Graduate Degree(s)

- Master of Architecture (M.Arch.)

Portfolio Requirement

There is no portfolio requirement for first-year applicants. Students are evaluated based on their high school GPA and SAT/ACT scores. Students must apply for continued admission into the upper division portion of the architecture program after their first year.

Scholarships Offered

The Edward & Yvonne Harvey Scholarship offers full tuition to architecture students with a 3.0+ GPA and who have demonstrated financial need. Other scholarships include the Fred Manis Scholarship in Architecture that awards $2500, the Jeffrey C. Landis Travel Scholarship that awards $3,500 for international travel for B.Arch. students, the John N. Cryer III-Page Scholarship ($2000), and more.

Special Opportunities

According to LSU, "[although] College of Art & Design students make up three percent of the university's student body, our students are responsible for 25 percent of the university's international travel". Students may study abroad in various academic programs abroad set up by the LSU faculty. Locations include Ireland, Italy, Vietnam, Germany, the UK, the Netherlands, and South Africa.

Notable Alumni

Hugh Griffin Parker, Jr.

TULANE UNIVERSITY

Address: 6823 St. Charles Ave., New Orleans, LA 70118
Website: *https://architecture.tulane.edu/*
Contact: *https://architecture.tulane.edu/contact-form*
Phone: (504) 865-5389
Email: undergrad.admission@tulane.edu

COST OF ATTENDANCE:

Tuition & Fees: $60,814 | **Additional Expenses:** $18,828
Total: $80,232

Financial Aid: https://admission.tulane.edu/tuition-aid

ADDITIONAL INFORMATION:

Available Degree(s)

- B.S. Architecture
- Bachelor of Architecture (B.Arch.) - 5-year

Portfolio Requirement

Although portfolios are not strictly required they are strongly encouraged for architecture applicants. In addition, students who are applying ED or EA, indicate Architecture as their first or second major, and submit a digital portfolio may be considered for the $10,000 Architecture Portfolio Award. Submit via Tulane's Green Wave Portal. Do not send architectural drafting work.

Scholarships Offered

The Architecture Portfolio Award ($10,000) is available. See above for details. In addition, full tuition, total-cost, and Louisiana resident scholarships are available, including the Deans' Honor Scholarship (DHS), the Paul Tulane Award, and the Stamps Scholarship.

Special Opportunities

The School of Architecture is housed in a 113-year-old building called Richardson Memorial Hall. This building will undergo renovation and open again in fall 2023. The construction will also serve as a teaching tool for students.

Notable Alumni

Nathaniel C. Curtis, Arthur Q. Davis, Robert Ivy, Albert C. Ledner, Bernard Lemann, Moise H. Goldstein, Sr., Jing Liu, Edward F. Neild, Willington "Duke" Reiter, Henry Hobson Richardson, A. Hays Town, and Samuel Wilson, Jr.

ALABAMA
ARKANSAS
DELAWARE
DISTRICT OF COLUMBIA
FLORIDA
GEORGIA
KENTUCKY
LOUISIANA
MARYLAND
MISSISSIPPI
NORTH CAROLINA
OKLAHOMA
SOUTH CAROLINA
TENNESSEE
TEXAS
VIRGINIA
WEST VIRGINIA

SOUTH

ALABAMA

ARKANSAS

DELAWARE

DISTRICT OF
COLUMBIA

FLORIDA

GEORGIA

KENTUCKY

LOUISIANA

MARYLAND

MISSISSIPPI

NORTH CAROLINA

OKLAHOMA

SOUTH CAROLINA

TENNESSEE

TEXAS

VIRGINIA

WEST VIRGINIA

NORTH CAROLINA STATE UNIVERSITY (NC STATE)

Address: 50 Pullen Road, Raleigh, NC 27695
Website: *https://design.ncsu.edu/*
Contact: *https://admissions.ncsu.edu/connect/*
Phone: (919) 515-2434
Email: undergrad-admissions@ncsu.edu

COST OF ATTENDANCE:

In-State Tuition & Fees: $9,128 | **Additional Expenses:** $16,624
Total: $25,752

Out-of-State Tuition & Fees: $30,869 | **Additional Expenses:** $16,888
Total: $47,757

Financial Aid: https://studentservices.ncsu.edu/your-money/financial-aid/

ADDITIONAL INFORMATION:

Available Degree(s)
- Bachelor of Environmental Design (B.E.D.A.)
- Bachelor of Architecture (B.Arch.) - 1-year*

Graduate Degree(s)
- Master of Architecture (M.Arch.)
- Master of Advanced Architectural Studies (M.A.A.S.)

Portfolio Requirement

Portfolios are required for first-year applicants. Submit via SlideRoom. The portfolio must include 10 images that demonstrate a range of mediums including titles and descriptions for each.

Scholarships Offered

The AIA Piedmont Section Scholarship, the Boney Architects Endowed Scholarship, the C.T. Wilson Scholarship, and several others are intended for architecture students with varying award amounts.

Special Opportunities

*Please note that the B.Arch. program is only available to students who already possess their four-year undergraduate degree in architecture. NCSU only offers first-years the Bachelor of Environmental Design in Architecture (BEDA). Once the student has their BEDA, they may be eligible for the one-year B.Arch. program or the two-year M.Arch.program.

Students may specialize in: City Design Certificate; Coastal Dynamics Design Lab; Design Build; Energy + Technology Certificate; History + Theory; Public Interest Design Certificate; Public Interest Design Studios.

Notable Alumni

Henry E. Bonitz and Brett Claywell

UNIVERSITY OF NORTH CAROLINA AT CHARLOTTE

Address: 9201 University City Boulevard, Charlotte, NC 28223
Website: *https://coaa.uncc.edu/architecture*
Contact: *https://admissions.charlotte.edu/admissions-counselors*
Phone: (704) 687-5507
Email: admissions@uncc.edu

COST OF ATTENDANCE:

In-State Tuition & Fees: $7,188 | **Additional Expenses:** $16,528
Total: $23,716

Out-of-State Tuition & Fees: $20,622 | **Additional Expenses:** $17,436
Total: $38,058

Financial Aid: https://www.uncc.edu/landing/admissions-financial-aid

ADDITIONAL INFORMATION:

Available Degree(s)

- B.A. Architecture

Graduate Degree(s)

- Master of Architecture (M.Arch.)
- Master of Urban Design (M.U.D.)
- M.S. Architecture

Portfolio Requirement

Portfolios are required. Students may be selected for an interview. This consists of a 30-minute interview where the applicants discuss their portfolio work. For the portfolio, mechanically-drafted/computer-based drawings may be included only if the work demonstrates personal creativity.

Scholarships Offered

Several merit-based and need-based scholarship opportunities for architecture students, including the AIA Charlotte Scholarship ($2000), the LS3P College of Architecture Scholarship ($2500), the Frederick J. Gregory Scholarship ($2000), etc.

Special Opportunities

Students are encouraged to study abroad through spring/summer study abroad, international exchanges, or fellowships. Furthermore, students may apply to the Arts and Architecture Honors Program (AAHP). The AAHP offers honors housing, an advisor, and research/travel grants. Additionally, UNC Charlotte B.Arch. graduates may be considered for advanced standing in the M.Arch. program.

Notable Alumni

John Barrett, Bryan Cantley, Je'Nen Chastain, Jamie Dail, Evan Danchenka, Chris Ford, Dennis Hall, Tarik Hameed, Jason Jones, Craig Kerins, Charlotte Lamb, Jeffrey Ludlow, Albert McDonald, Zachary Tate Porter, David Ravin, Cherish Rosas, Terry Shook, and Elizabeth Unruh

ALABAMA

ARKANSAS

DELAWARE

DISTRICT OF COLUMBIA

FLORIDA

GEORGIA

KENTUCKY

LOUISIANA

MARYLAND

MISSISSIPPI

NORTH CAROLINA

OKLAHOMA

SOUTH CAROLINA

TENNESSEE

TEXAS

VIRGINIA

WEST VIRGINIA

SOUTH

ALABAMA

ARKANSAS

DELAWARE

DISTRICT OF
COLUMBIA

FLORIDA

GEORGIA

KENTUCKY

LOUISIANA

MARYLAND

MISSISSIPPI

NORTH CAROLINA

OKLAHOMA

SOUTH CAROLINA

TENNESSEE

TEXAS

VIRGINIA

WEST VIRGINIA

OKLAHOMA STATE UNIVERSITY

Address: Oklahoma State University, Stillwater, OK 74078
Website: *https://ceat.okstate.edu/*
Contact: *https://go.okstate.edu/admissions/contact-us.html*
Phone: (405) 744-5140
Email: admissions@okstate.edu

COST OF ATTENDANCE:

In-State Tuition & Fees: $13,920 | **Additional Expenses:** $15,970
Total: $29,890

Out-of-State Tuition & Fees: $29,440 | **Additional Expenses:** $15,970
Total: $45,410

Financial Aid: https://go.okstate.edu/scholarships-financial-aid/

ADDITIONAL INFORMATION:

Available Degree(s)

- Bachelor of Architecture (B.Arch.) - 5-year
- Bachelor of Architectural Engineering - 5-year

Portfolio Requirement

There is no portfolio requirement. Oklahoma State School of Architecture has an open enrollment policy for the first two years of the architecture program. As long as the applicant meets the university requirements and there is space, they will be admitted. However, after the first two years, the student must apply to the professional program. Selection is based on completion of the required credit hours, specific courses, and a minimum 2.8 GPA.

Scholarships Offered

The Allen Scholars Program offers undergraduate architecture students $7,500 each year for up to four years. In addition, the W.W. Allen Boys and Girls Club Program offers architecture students $15,000 annually.

Special Opportunities

Oklahoma State requires architecture students to partake in a one-month study abroad experience in Europe or Asia.

Notable Alumni

Randall Heckenkemper and Jerry Slack

UNIVERSITY OF OKLAHOMA

Address: 830 Van Vleet Oval, Norman, OK 73019
Website: *https://architecture.ou.edu/*
Contact: *http://www.ou.edu/web/about_ou/contact*
Phone: (405) 325-2444
Email: admissions@ou.edu

COST OF ATTENDANCE:

In-State Tuition & Fees: $13,065 | **Additional Expenses:** $19,350
Total: $32,415

Out-of-State Tuition & Fees: $28,869 | **Additional Expenses:** $19,350
Total: $48,219

Financial Aid: http://www.ou.edu/admissions/affordability/
financial-aid

ADDITIONAL INFORMATION:

Available Degree(s)

- Bachelor of Architecture (B.Arch.) - 5-year
- Bachelor of Construction Science
- B.S. Environmental Design
- B.S. Architectural Studies (B.S.A.S.)
- Bachelor of Interior Design

Graduate Degree(s)

- Master of Architecture (M.Arch.)
- Master of Landscape Architectural Studies
- Master of Urban Design
- M.S. Planning, Design, and Construction
- Ph.D. Planning, Design, and Construction

Portfolio Requirement

Portfolios are not required.

Scholarships Offered

The Award of Excellence ($16,000), Distinguished Scholar ($12,000),
University Scholarship ($10,000), and other scholarships are
available.

Special Opportunities

Students have the option to participate in Travel Study. Faculty
sometimes accompanies students to certain locations, such as
the trip to Uganda. In this program, students learn to support
peace-building efforts. Other locations include Italy, Chicago, China,
Zambia, and numerous other places.

Notable Alumni

Mohammad Farzaneh, Jalal Farzaneh, and Gina Sofola

ALABAMA

ARKANSAS

DELAWARE

DISTRICT OF
COLUMBIA

FLORIDA

GEORGIA

KENTUCKY

LOUISIANA

MARYLAND

MISSISSIPPI

NORTH CAROLINA

OKLAHOMA

SOUTH CAROLINA

TENNESSEE

TEXAS

VIRGINIA

WEST VIRGINIA

SOUTH

THE UNIVERSITY OF TENNESSEE, KNOXVILLE

Address: 1715 Volunteer Blvd, Knoxville, TN 37996
Website: *https://archdesign.utk.edu/*
Contact: *https://admissions.utk.edu/more-information/getting-in-touch*
Phone: (865) 974-1111
Email: onestop@utk.edu

COST OF ATTENDANCE:

In-State Tuition & Fees: $13,264 | **Additional Expenses:** $19,234
Total: $32,498

Out-of-State Tuition & Fees: $31,684 | **Additional Expenses:** $19,234
Total: $50,918

Financial Aid: https://onestop.utk.edu/financial-aid/

ADDITIONAL INFORMATION:

Available Degree(s)

- Bachelor of Architecture (B.Arch.) - 5-year
- B.S. Interior Architecture

Graduate Degree(s)

- Master of Architecture (M.Arch.)
- Master of Landscape Architecture (M.L.A.)

Portfolio Requirement

Applicants are strongly encouraged to apply by the School of Architecture priority deadline of November 1. Students who apply by this date are considered for competitive scholarships. Portfolios are optional but strongly recommended. Applicants should submit their portfolio via the VIP Portal.

Scholarships Offered

Chancellor's Scholarships are merit-based aid awarded to incoming students. The minimum requirement is an ACT score of 31, SAT of 1390, and 4.0+ GPA. Some of these scholarships award $5,000 per year for four years or $7,000 per year for four years. In addition, the HOPE (Lottery) Scholarship is available to TN residents.There are various scholarships specific to architecture students as well.

Special Opportunities

There are numerous dual degree opportunities, such as the 5+1 B.Arch./M.L.A., 4+2 B.S. Interior Architecture/M.Arch., 4-year M.Arch./M.L.A., or the 4+2 B.S. Interior Architecture/M.L.A.

Notable Alumni

Robin Klehr Avia, Patrick Hazari, and Darris James

ALABAMA

ARKANSAS

DELAWARE

DISTRICT OF COLUMBIA

FLORIDA

GEORGIA

KENTUCKY

LOUISIANA

MARYLAND

MISSISSIPPI

NORTH CAROLINA

OKLAHOMA

SOUTH CAROLINA

TENNESSEE

TEXAS

VIRGINIA

WEST VIRGINIA

RICE UNIVERSITY

Address: 6100 Main Street, Houston, TX 77005
Website: *https://arch.rice.edu/*
Contact: *See bottom of page - https://admission.rice.edu/*
Phone: (713) 348-4864
Email: admission@rice.edu

COST OF ATTENDANCE:

Tuition & Fees: $52,895 | **Additional Expenses:** $18,850
Total: $71,745

Financial Aid: https://arch.rice.edu/apply/financial-aid

ADDITIONAL INFORMATION:

Available Degree(s)

- B.A. Architecture/Bachelor of Architecture (B.Arch.) - 6-year dual degree

Portfolio Requirement

Portfolios are required for incoming students. Submit via Rice Admission Student Portal. Include up to 10 pages, more than one work can be included per page. Do not include drafting or CAD drawings.

Scholarships Offered

Rice University offers a generous need-based aid package to students. Students whose family income is $75,000 or below receive a grant for full tuition, fees, and room and board. Students whose family income is $75,000-140,000 receive a grant for full tuition. Students whose family income is $140,000-$200,000 receive a grant for half tuition.

Special Opportunities

Rice Architecture offers two consecutive degrees: four years for a B.A.in Architecture, then a B.Arch. after two more years. When students apply, they are applying for a five-year B.Arch. program with a "bonus" Preceptorship year, for a total of six years. The preceptorship year places B.Arch. students at offices across the world. Students must pass certain checkpoints at the end of sophomore year and in the middle of senior year to proceed in the program. Advanced B.Arch. students may complete a semester-long study abroad term at Rice Architecture Paris.

Notable Alumni

Karen Cook, E. Fay Jones, Eric Kuhne, and Charles Renfro

ALABAMA
ARKANSAS
DELAWARE
DISTRICT OF COLUMBIA
FLORIDA
GEORGIA
KENTUCKY
LOUISIANA
MARYLAND
MISSISSIPPI
NORTH CAROLINA
OKLAHOMA
SOUTH CAROLINA
TENNESSEE
TEXAS
VIRGINIA
WEST VIRGINIA

SOUTH

ALABAMA

ARKANSAS

DELAWARE

DISTRICT OF
COLUMBIA

FLORIDA

GEORGIA

KENTUCKY

LOUISIANA

MARYLAND

MISSISSIPPI

NORTH CAROLINA

OKLAHOMA

SOUTH CAROLINA

TENNESSEE

TEXAS

VIRGINIA

WEST VIRGINIA

TEXAS A&M UNIVERSITY

Address: 400 Bizzell St, College Station, TX 77843
Website: *https://www.arch.tamu.edu/academics/undergraduate-programs/majors/*
Contact: *http://www.arch.tamu.edu/contact/*
Phone: (979) 845-1060
Email: admissions@tamu.edu

COST OF ATTENDANCE:

In-State Tuition & Fees: $13,012 | **Additional Expenses:** $19,014
Total: $32,026

Out-of-State Tuition & Fees: $40,896 | **Additional Expenses:** $20,414
Total: $61,310

Financial Aid: https://financialaid.tamu.edu/

ADDITIONAL INFORMATION:

Available Degree(s)
- Bachelor of Landscape Architecture (B.L.A.)
- B.S. Environmental Design
- B.S. Construction Science
- B.S. Urban and Regional Planning
- B.S. Visualization

Graduate Degree(s)
- Master of Architecture (M.Arch.)
- M.S. Architecture
- M.S. Land & Property Development
- M.S. Landscape Architecture
- M.S. Urban Planning
- Ph.D. Architecture
- Ph.D. Construction Science
- Ph.D. Urban and Regional Sciences

Portfolio Requirement
There is no portfolio requirement for freshmen applicants.

Scholarships Offered
Texas A&M's Academic Scholarships are available to incoming freshmen for fall admission. Some scholarships include the President's Endowed Scholarship ($3000 per year for 4 years), the Lechner Scholarship ($2500 per year for 4 years), and the McFadden Scholarship ($2500 per year for 4 years). Texas A&M also offers various academic achievement scholarships, awards for out-of-state students, and many others. All undergraduate and graduate College of Architecture students are considered for architecture scholarships. No scholarship application is required.

Special Opportunities
The Bachelors in Environmental Design is a studio-based program preparing students for the M.Arch. Visualization offers studio-based classes integrating 3D design & digital architecture technology.

Notable Alumni
Nestor Bottino, Caren Cooner Easterling, Anat Geva, Tushar Gupta, Todd C. Howard, Jean-Claude Kalache, Brian Peter Kraleyvich, Thomas McKittrick, Tim McLaughlin, David Preziosi, Michelle Robinson, Adrian Smith, Lorena Tellez Toffer, and Shannon Van Zandt

UNIVERSITY OF HOUSTON

Address: 4200 Elgin Street, Room 122, Houston, TX 77204
Website: *https://www.uh.edu/architecture/*
Contact: *https://www.uh.edu/architecture/contacts/*
Phone: (713) 743-2400
Email: admissions@uh.edu

COST OF ATTENDANCE:

In-State Tuition & Fees: $11,569 | **Additional Expenses:** $11,110
Total: $22,679

Out-of-State Tuition & Fees: $26,839 | **Additional Expenses:** $11,110
Total: $37,949

Financial Aid: https://uh.edu/undergraduate-admissions/cost/index.php

ADDITIONAL INFORMATION:

Available Degree(s)

- Bachelor of Architecture (B.Arch.) - 5-year
- B.S. Interior Architecture
- B.S. Industrial Design
- B.S. Environmental Design

Graduate Degree(s)

- Master of Architecture (M.Arch.)
- M.A. Architectural Studies
- M.S. Architecture
- M.S. Industrial Design

Portfolio Requirement

Applicants are strongly encouraged to submit a portfolio. Submit via University of Houston website. Include 8-10 examples of work, including drawings, sculptures, ceramics, dance performance, architectural drawings, etc.

Scholarships Offered

Gerald D. Hines College of Architecture and Design Scholarship awards range from $500-$2000. In addition, university scholarships based on merit and/or demonstrated need are available to all students. For instance, the Academic Excellence scholarship gifts an award of up to $6,000 per year.

Special Opportunities

Study abroad is available to the College of Architecture and Design students. There are faculty-led and exchange programs. Locations include Austria, Chile, Italy, Spain, India, and several other destinations. Students must apply for these programs and submit a portfolio.

Notable Alumni

Neil Denari, Burdette Keeland, Jr., and Jerrold E. Lomax

ALABAMA
ARKANSAS
DELAWARE
DISTRICT OF COLUMBIA
FLORIDA
GEORGIA
KENTUCKY
LOUISIANA
MARYLAND
MISSISSIPPI
NORTH CAROLINA
OKLAHOMA
SOUTH CAROLINA
TENNESSEE
TEXAS
VIRGINIA
WEST VIRGINIA

SOUTH

THE UNIVERSITY OF TEXAS AT AUSTIN (UT AUSTIN)

Address: 310 Inner Campus Drive, Austin, TX 78712
Website: *https://archdesign.caus.vt.edu/*
Contact: *https://admissions.utexas.edu/contact*
Phone: (512) 471-1922
Email: admissions@austin.utexas.edu

COST OF ATTENDANCE:

In-State Tuition & Fees: $10,824 | **Additional Expenses:** $16,904
Total: $27,728

Out-of-State Tuition & Fees: $38,326 | **Additional Expenses:** $16,904
Total: $55,230

Financial Aid: https://finaid.utexas.edu/

ADDITIONAL INFORMATION:

Available Degree(s)

- Bachelor of Architecture (B.Arch.)
- B.S. Architectural Studies (B.S.A.S.)
- B.S. Interior Design
- B.S. Architectural Engineering

Graduate Degree(s)

- Master of Architecture (M.Arch.)
- Master of Interior Design

Portfolio Requirement

Portfolios are not required nor accepted for first-year applicants.

Scholarships Offered

The School of Architecture gifts continuing architecture students scholarships with amounts ranging from $500 to $5000.

Special opportunities

Students are encouraged to study abroad. UT Austin offers numerous opportunities for students to learn more about international architectural structures. UT Austin offers an Architecture in Europe Program, where students spend fall semester studying buildings and landscapes across Europe. Another option is Studio Mexico, a nine-day trip during spring semester to visit design project sites. In addition, Advanced Studios offers opportunities to travel abroad to locations such as Brazil, Ecuador, France, Iceland, Japan, and other destinations. Summer Faculty-led Programs are six to nine-week study abroad programs that are also available.

Notable Alumni

Howard Barr, John Chase, Craig Dykers, Everett Fly, Tom Kite, David Lake, Elaine Molinar, and Fernando Belaúnde Terry

ALABAMA

ARKANSAS

DELAWARE

DISTRICT OF COLUMBIA

FLORIDA

GEORGIA

KENTUCKY

LOUISIANA

MARYLAND

MISSISSIPPI

NORTH CAROLINA

OKLAHOMA

SOUTH CAROLINA

TENNESSEE

TEXAS

VIRGINIA

WEST VIRGINIA

UNIVERSITY OF VIRGINIA

Address: University of Virginia, Charlottesville, VA 22904
Website: *https://www.arch.virginia.edu/programs/architecture/undergraduate*
Contact: *https://admission.virginia.edu/connect*
Phone: (434) 982-3200
Email: undergradadmission@virginia.edu

COST OF ATTENDANCE:

In-State Tuition & Fees: $18,516 | **Additional Expenses:** $17,142
Total: $35,658

Out-of-State Tuition & Fees: $53,084 | **Additional Expenses:** $18,615
Total: $71,699

Financial Aid: https://sfs.virginia.edu/

ADDITIONAL INFORMATION:

Available Degree(s)

- B.S. Architecture
- Bachelor of Architectural History
- Bachelor of Urban and Environmental Planning

Portfolio Requirement

There is no portfolio requirement for first-year applicants.

Scholarships Offered

University of Virginia offers endowed, need-based scholarships to students. In most cases, students do not need to submit a separate application for consideration. Students may also apply for non-UVA scholarships.

Special Opportunities

In the first year, architecture students must take core courses in three departments: Architecture, Urban & Environmental Planning, and Architectural History. At the end of the first year, students then decide which major they would like to pursue. Furthermore, high-performing undergraduates may gain direct admission to a graduate program within the School of Architecture. All undergraduates with a cumulative GPA of 3.3+ are assured direct admission and advanced standing into a graduate program. UVA offers 4+1, 4+2, and 4+2.5 tracks depending on the choice of the degree.

Notable Alumni

Kai-Uwe Bergmann, Warren T. Byrd, Jr., Bill Hellmuth, Jennifer Masengarb, Travis C. McDonald, W. Brown Morton, III, Reuben M. Rainey, Marion Weiss, Mabel O. Wilson, and Adam Yarinsky

ALABAMA
ARKANSAS
DELAWARE
DISTRICT OF COLUMBIA
FLORIDA
GEORGIA
KENTUCKY
LOUISIANA
MARYLAND
MISSISSIPPI
NORTH CAROLINA
OKLAHOMA
SOUTH CAROLINA
TENNESSEE
TEXAS
VIRGINIA
WEST VIRGINIA

SOUTH

VIRGINIA POLYTECHNIC STATE UNIVERSITY

Address: 1325 Perry Street, Blacksburg, VA 24061
Website: *https://archdesign.caus.vt.edu/*
Contact: *https://archdesign.caus.vt.edu/contact/*
Phone: (540) 231-5383
Email: admissions@vt.edu

COST OF ATTENDANCE:

In-State Tuition & Fees: $14,586 | **Additional Expenses:** $17,688
Total: $32,274

Out-of-State Tuition & Fees: $34,838 | **Additional Expenses:** $17,920
Total: $52,758

Financial Aid: https://vt.edu/admissions/undergraduate/cost.html

ADDITIONAL INFORMATION:

Available Degree(s)

- Bachelor of Architecture (B.Arch.) - 5-year
- B.S. Industrial Design
- B.S. Interior Design
- Bachelor of Landscape Architecture (B.L.A.)

Graduate Degree(s)

- Master of Architecture (M.Arch.)
- Master of Landscape Architecture (M.L.A.)
- M.S. Architecture, concentrations: Building Science; Urban Design

Portfolio Requirement

Portfolios are not required for first-year applicants.

Scholarships Offered

Virginia Tech offers scholarships specific to architecture students. These scholarships have varying amounts and requirements to fulfill. Scholarships include the A+D Annual Scholarship Fund, the Hazel-Pruitt Scholarship, the Charles S. Worley Scholarship, and more.

Notable Alumni

Martin Felsen, Kevin Jones, and Charles W. Steger

ALABAMA

ARKANSAS

DELAWARE

DISTRICT OF COLUMBIA

FLORIDA

GEORGIA

KENTUCKY

LOUISIANA

MARYLAND

MISSISSIPPI

NORTH CAROLINA

OKLAHOMA

SOUTH CAROLINA

TENNESSEE

TEXAS

VIRGINIA

WEST VIRGINIA

ALASKA

ARIZONA

CALIFORNIA

COLORADO

HAWAII

IDAHO

MONTANA

NEVADA

NEW MEXICO

OREGON

UTAH

WASHINGTON

WYOMING

CHAPTER 14

REGION FOUR

WEST

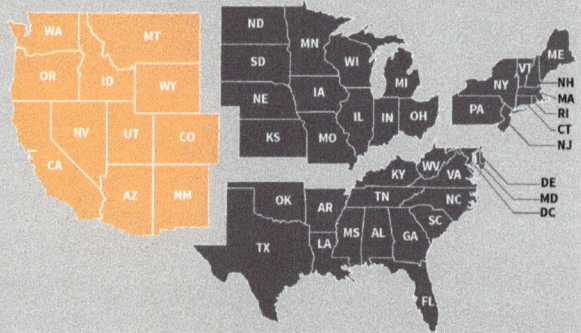

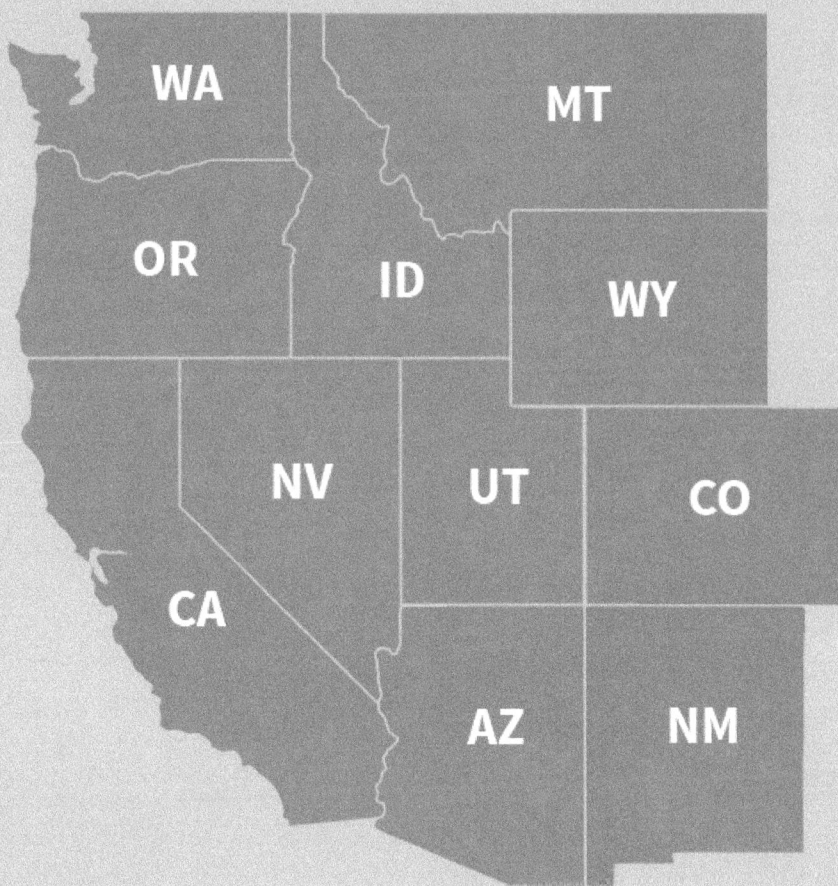

10 Programs | 13 States

1. AZ – University of Arizona
2. CA - California State Polytechnic University, Pomona (Cal Poly Pomona)
3. CA - California Polytechnic State University, San Luis Obispo (Cal Poly SLO)
4. CA - California College of the Arts (CCA)
5. CA - Southern California Institute of Architecture (SCI-Arc)
6. CA - University of California, Berkeley
7. CA - University of California, Los Angeles (UCLA)
8. CA - University of Southern California (USC)
9. OR - University of Oregon
10. WA - University of Washington

ARCHITECTURE PROGRAMS

School	Avg. GPA, SAT Evidence-Based Reading Writing (ERW), SAT Math (M), and ACT Composite (C) Early Decision (ED): Yes/No	Admission Statistics	Program(s)	Portfolio Required (req.)
University of Arizona 1040 N. Olive Rd., Tucson, AZ 85721	GPA: 3.43 SAT (ERW): 550-660 SAT (M): 540-690 ACT (C): 21-29 ED: No	Overall College Admit Rate: 85% Undergrad Enrollment: 36,503 Total Enrollment: 46,932	Bachelor of Architecture (B.Arch.) - 5-year Bachelor of Landscape Architecture (B.L.A.) B.S. Sustainable Built Environments Graduate Degree(s): Master of Architecture (M.Arch.) M.S. Architecture Master of Landscape Architecture (M.L.A.) Master of Real Estate Development M.S. Urban Planning Degrees Awarded in the Program(s): 155	Portfolio not req.

School	Avg. GPA, SAT Evidence-Based Reading Writing (ERW), SAT Math (M), and ACT Composite (C) / Early Decision (ED): Yes/No	Admission Statistics	Program(s)	Portfolio Required (req.)
California State Polytechnic University, Pomona (Cal Poly Pomona) 3801 West Temple Avenue, Pomona, CA 91768	GPA: N/A SAT (ERW): 500-610 SAT (M): 510-640 ACT (C): 19-27 ED: No	Overall College Admit Rate: 65% Undergrad Enrollment: 27,912 Total Enrollment: 30,014	Bachelor of Architecture (B.Arch.) - 5-year B.S. Landscape Architecture (B.S.L.A.) Graduate Degree(s): Master of Architecture (M.Arch.) Master of Interior Architecture Master of Landscape Architecture (M.L.A.) Degrees Awarded in the Program(s): 183	Portfolio not req.
California Polytechnic State University, San Luis Obispo (Cal Poly SLO) 1 Grand Avenue, San Luis Obispo, CA 93407	GPA: 3.99 SAT (ERW): 610-690 SAT (M): 610-720 ACT (C): 26-32 ED: No	Overall College Admit Rate: 38% Undergrad Enrollment: 21,456 Total Enrollment: 22,440	Bachelor of Architecture (B.Arch.) - 5-year Degrees Awarded in the Program(s): 200	Portfolio not req.

WEST

School	Avg. GPA, SAT Evidence-Based Reading Writing (ERW), SAT Math (M), and ACT Composite (C) Early Decision (ED): Yes/No	Admission Statistics	Program(s)	Portfolio Required (req.)
California College of the Arts (CCA) 1111 Eighth St., San Francisco, CA 94107	GPA: N/A SAT (ERW): N/A* SAT (M): N/A* ACT (C): N/A* *Test-optional ED: No	Overall College Admit Rate: 85% Undergrad Enrollment: 1,239 Total Enrollment: 1,612	Bachelor of Architecture (B.Arch.) - 5-year BFA Interior Design Graduate Degree(s): Master of Architecture (M.Arch.) Master of Advanced Architectural Design (M.A.A.D.) Degrees Awarded in the Program(s): 26	Portfolio req.
Southern California Institute of Architecture (SCI-Arc) 960 East 3rd Street, Los Angeles, CA 90013	GPA: N/A SAT (ERW): 499-651 SAT (M): 500-685 ACT (C): 27-30 ED: No	Overall College Admit Rate: 67% Undergrad Enrollment: 249 Total Enrollment: 481	Bachelor of Architecture (B.Arch.) - 5-year Graduate Degree(s): Master of Architecture (M.Arch.) Degrees Awarded in the Program(s): 49	Portfolio optional

School	Avg. GPA, SAT Evidence-Based Reading Writing (ERW), SAT Math (M), and ACT Composite (C) Early Decision (ED): Yes/No	Admission Statistics	Program(s)	Portfolio Required (req.)
University of California, Berkeley University of California, Berkeley, Berkeley, CA 94720	GPA: 3.87 SAT (ERW): 650-740 SAT (M): 660-790 ACT (C): 30-35 ED: No	Overall College Admit Rate: 17% Undergrad Enrollment: 30,799 Total Enrollment: 42,327	B.A. Architecture Graduate Degree(s): Master of Architecture (M.Arch.) Master of Advanced Architectural Design (M.A.A.D) M.S. Architecture Ph.D. Architecture Degrees Awarded in the Program(s): 142	Portfolio not req.
University of California, Los Angeles (UCLA) 405 Hilgard Avenue, Los Angeles, CA 90095	GPA: 3.9 SAT (ERW): 650-740 SAT (M): 640-780 ACT (C): 29-34 ED: No	Overall College Admit Rate: 14% Undergrad Enrollment: 31,636 Total Enrollment: 44,589	B.A. Architectural Studies - 2-year Graduate Degree(s): Master of Architecture (M.Arch.) M.S. Architecture and Urban Design M.A./Ph.D. Architecture Degrees Awarded in the Program(s): 21	Portfolio not req.

WEST

School	Avg. GPA, SAT Evidence-Based Reading Writing (ERW), SAT Math (M), and ACT Composite (C) Early Decision (ED): Yes/No	Admission Statistics	Program(s)	Portfolio Required (req.)
University of Southern California (USC) Watt Hall, Suite 204, Los Angeles, CA 90089	GPA: 3.83 SAT (ERW): 660-740 SAT (M): 680-790 ACT (C): 30-34 ED: No	Overall College Admit Rate: 16% Undergrad Enrollment: 19,786 Total Enrollment: 46,287	B.A. Architecture Bachelor of Architecture (B.Arch.) - 5-year Graduate Degree(s): Master of Advanced Architectural Studies (M.A.A.S.) Master of Building Science (M.B.S.) Degrees Awarded in the Program(s): 206	Portfolio not req.

School	Avg. GPA, SAT Evidence-Based Reading Writing (ERW), SAT Math (M), and ACT Composite (C) Early Decision (ED): Yes/No	Admission Statistics	Program(s)	Portfolio Required (req.)
University of Oregon 5249 University of Oregon, Eugene, OR 97403	GPA: 3.65 SAT (ERW): 550-650 SAT (M): 540-640 ACT (C): 22-29 ED: No	Overall College Admit Rate: 84% Undergrad Enrollment: 18,045 Total Enrollment: 21,752	Bachelor of Architecture (B.Arch.) - 5-year Bachelor of Landscape Architecture (B.L.A.) Bachelor of Interior Architecture Graduate Degree(s): Master of Architecture (M.Arch.) M.S. Architecture Ph.D. Architecture Degrees Awarded in the Program(s): 77	Portfolio optional
University of Washington 1400 NE Campus Parkway, Seattle, WA, 98195	GPA: 3.82 SAT (ERW): 590-700 SAT (M): 610-753 ACT (C). 27-33 ED: No	Overall College Admit Rate: 56% Undergrad Enrollment: 32,244 Total Enrollment: 48,149	B.A. Architecture B.A. Architectural Design Degrees Awarded in the Program(s): 152	Portfolio req.

WEST

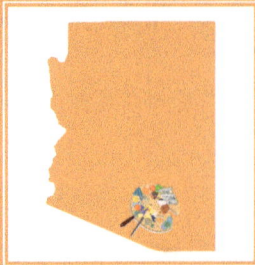

ALASKA

ARIZONA

CALIFORNIA

COLORADO

HAWAII

IDAHO

MONTANA

NEVADA

NEW MEXICO

OREGON

UTAH

WASHINGTON

WYOMING

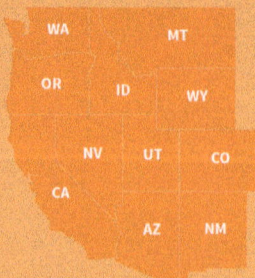

UNIVERSITY OF ARIZONA

Address: 1040 N. Olive Rd., Tucson, AZ 85721
Website: *https://capla.arizona.edu/*
Contact: *https://www.arizona.edu/contact-us*
Phone: (520) 621-6751
Email: admissions@arizona.edu

COST OF ATTENDANCE:

In-State Tuition & Fees: $12,700 | **Additional Expenses:** $18,050
Total: $30,750

Out-of-State Tuition & Fees: $37,200 | **Additional Expenses:** $18,050
Total: $55,250

Financial Aid: https://financialaid.arizona.edu/

ADDITIONAL INFORMATION:

Available Degree(s)

- Bachelor of Architecture (B.Arch.) - 5-year
- Bachelor of Landscape Architecture (B.L.A.)
- B.S. Sustainable Built Environments

Graduate Degree(s)

- Master of Architecture (M.Arch.)
- M.S. Architecture
- Master of Landscape Architecture (M.L.A.)
- Master of Real Estate Development
- M.S. Urban Planning

Portfolio Requirement

Portfolios are not required for first-year applicants.

Scholarships Offered

University of Arizona offers several merit-based and need-based awards. Arizona residents are eligible for the Resident Wildcat Awards, based on GPA and test scores. Awards range from $3,000-$15,000. The Non-Resident Arizona Awards range from $2,000-$35,000.

Special Opportunities

Study abroad opportunities are available. Students may accompany faculty to various programs in Latin American Europe, Asia, and Africa. In addition, students may enroll directly to an institution abroad or another program hosted by another Arizona college. Students may minor in Architectural History & Theory, Real Estate Development, Landscape Architecture, or Sustainable Built Environments.

Notable Alumni

Richard Altuna, Dan Heinfeld, Heather Henricks, Rich Michal, Dyron Murphy, Roy Noggle, Gustavo Antonio Noriega, David D. Ortega, Lawrence G. Paull, Georgia Pennington, Lena Porell, and Adriana Zuniga

CALIFORNIA STATE POLYTECHNIC UNIVERSITY, POMONA (CAL POLY POMONA)

Address: 3801 West Temple Avenue, Pomona, CA 91768
Website: *http://env.cpp.edu/env/env*
Contact: *http://env.cpp.edu/env/contact-env*
Phone: (909) 869-5299
Email: admissions@cpp.edu

COST OF ATTENDANCE:

In-State Tuition & Fees: $7,438 | **Additional Expenses:** $20,578
Total: $28,016

Out-of-State Tuition & Fees: $19,318 | **Additional Expenses:** $20,578
Total: $39,896

Financial Aid: https://www.cpp.edu/financial-aid/index.shtml

ADDITIONAL INFORMATION:

Available Degree(s)
- Bachelor of Architecture (B.Arch.) - 5-year
- B.S. Landscape Architecture (B.S.L.A.)

Graduate Degree(s)
- Master of Architecture (M.Arch.)
- Master of Interior Architecture
- Master of Landscape Architecture (M.L.A.)

Portfolio Requirement
Portfolios are not required for applicants. The B.Arch. degree is an impacted program, therefore far more students apply than can be accommodated. Cal Poly Pomona has "local area admission preference", meaning that applicants outside of the designated local area will be held to higher admission standards.

Scholarships Offered
The Department of Landscape Architecture offers more than $50,000 annually through scholarships. In addition, they recommend applying to external scholarships such as the AWA + D Scholarships, the Landscape Architecture Foundation, and the American Society of Landscape Architects Scholarships and Fellowships. Cal Poly Pomona also has a Scholarship Fest application cycle that runs from October 1st through March 2nd. Students must apply via the Bronco Scholarship Portal.

Special Opportunities
Students may enjoy studying abroad at various architecture programs in Europe, Asia, and Latin America. Furthermore, fourth-year architecture students may go on a year-long study abroad trip sponsored by California State University International Programs.

Notable Alumni
Mike Abbaté, Victoria Basolo, Frank O. Bostrom, Stan Braden, Gordon A. Bradley, W. Frank Brandt, Don Brinkerhoff, Robert R. Cardoza, Raymond K. Cheng, Earl Gales, Jr., Rebecca Hamm, James E. Hartl, Danielle Takata Herring, Mark G. Johnson, Robert J. Kain, Frank H. Kawasaki, Steven A. Preston, Cynthia Nelson, Dennis Y. Otsuji, Sanford Smith, Richard B. Stephens, Ming Tai, Danny Tisdale, Juliana Curran Terian, and Bob Weis

ALASKA

ARIZONA

CALIFORNIA

COLORADO

HAWAII

IDAHO

MONTANA

NEVADA

NEW MEXICO

OREGON

UTAH

WASHINGTON

WYOMING

WEST

ALASKA

ARIZONA

CALIFORNIA

COLORADO

HAWAII

IDAHO

MONTANA

NEVADA

NEW MEXICO

OREGON

UTAH

WASHINGTON

WYOMING

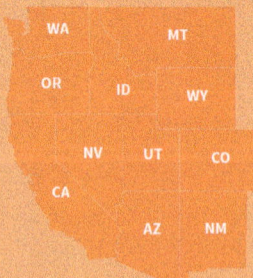

CALIFORNIA POLYTECHNIC STATE UNIVERSITY, SAN LUIS OBISPO (CAL POLY SLO)

Address: 1 Grand Avenue, San Luis Obispo, CA 93407
Website: *http://www.caed.calpoly.edu/*
Contact: *http://www.caed.calpoly.edu/content/people/index*
Phone: (805) 756-1311
Email: caed@calpoly.edu

COST OF ATTENDANCE:

In-State Tuition & Fees: $10,194 | **Additional Expenses:** $18,855
Total: $29,721

Out-of-State Tuition & Fees: $22,074 | **Additional Expenses:** $25,557
Total: $47,631

Financial Aid: https://www.calpoly.edu/tuition-and-financial-aid

ADDITIONAL INFORMATION:

Available Degree(s)

- Bachelor of Architecture (B.Arch.) - 5-year

Portfolio Requirement

Portfolios are not required for first-year applicants.

Scholarships Offered

The Architecture Department offers merit-based and need-based scholarships. Some scholarships include the Alfred B. Berghell & Joy G. Berghell Scholarship ($1200), the Alicia Daniels Uhlig Scholarship ($1800), and several others. Apply by March 30th for university scholarships and by April 30th for CAED Architecture Department scholarships. Need-based scholarships require the submission of a FAFSA.

Special Opportunities

CAED offers the Architecture Summer Career Workshop that includes hands-on modeling projects, small studios, and portfolio building. Cal Poly is one of the largest in the U.S. One in five architects in California and one in twenty in the U.S. graduated from Cal Poly SLO. Faculty-led programs are offered to Rome, Mexico, Japan, Switzerland, Thailand, and S.F. There are also exchange programs in Paris and D.C.

Notable Alumni

Irene Chan, Robert J. Condia, Milford Wayne Donaldson, Rebekah Gladson, Nathan L. Good, Paul Neel, and Lee E. Salin

CALIFORNIA COLLEGE OF THE ARTS (CCA)

Address: 1111 Eighth St., San Francisco, CA 94107
Website: *https://www.cca.edu/architecture/*
Contact: *Contact via phone or email.*
Phone: (800) 447-1278
Email: info@cca.edu

COST OF ATTENDANCE:

Tuition & Fees: $54,726 | **Additional Expenses:** $25,255
Total: $79,981

Financial Aid: https://www.cca.edu/admissions/tuition/#section-financial-aid

ADDITIONAL INFORMATION:

Available Degree(s)

- Bachelor of Architecture (B.Arch.) - 5-year
- BFA Interior Design

Graduate Degree(s)

- Master of Architecture (M.Arch.)
- Master of Advanced Architectural Design (M.A.A.D.)

Portfolio Requirement

Portfolios are required. Submit 10-15 works via SlideRoom.

Scholarships Offered

Merit-based, need-based, CCA-named, and other scholarships available.

Special Opportunities

Students may study abroad during the summer. The programs are led by CCA faculty and destinations are in European capitals and South Korea. Students may also participate in AICAD Exchange and study at one of the 31 participating schools around the country.

Notable Alumni

Gary Hutton, George Jewett, Tina Manis, Tim Perks, Hugo Steccati, Steven Utz, Kelly Walker, and Charly Wittock

ALASKA

ARIZONA

CALIFORNIA

COLORADO

HAWAII

IDAHO

MONTANA

NEVADA

NEW MEXICO

OREGON

UTAH

WASHINGTON

WYOMING

WEST

SOUTHERN CALIFORNIA INSTITUTE OF ARCHITECTURE (SCI-ARC)

Address: 960 East 3rd Street, Los Angeles, CA 90013
Website: *https://www.sciarc.edu/*
Contact: *Contact via phone or email.*
Phone: (213) 613-2200
Email: admissions@sciarc.edu

COST OF ATTENDANCE:

Tuition & Fees: $24,745 | **Additional Expenses:** $17,410
Total: $42,155

Financial Aid: https://www.sciarc.edu/admissions/financial-aid

ADDITIONAL INFORMATION:

Available Degree(s)

- Bachelor of Architecture (B.Arch.) - 5-year

Graduate Degree(s)

- Master of Architecture (M.Arch.)

Portfolio Requirement

Portfolios are optional. Submit 5-25 works via SlideRoom.

Scholarships Offered

The LAUSD Full-Tuition Scholarship is a merit-based scholarship available to LAUSD students.

Special Opportunities

High school students may participate in SCI-Arc's three-week immersive program, Design Immersion Days (DID).

Notable Alumni

Shigeru Ban, David Randall Hertz, and Mimi Zeiger

ALASKA

ARIZONA

CALIFORNIA

COLORADO

HAWAII

IDAHO

MONTANA

NEVADA

NEW MEXICO

OREGON

UTAH

WASHINGTON

WYOMING

UNIVERSITY OF CALIFORNIA, BERKELEY,

Address: University of California, Berkeley, Berkeley, CA 94720
Website: *https://ced.berkeley.edu/academics/architecture/programs/bachelor-of-arts-in-architecture*
Contact: *https://admissions.berkeley.edu/contact-us*
Phone: (510) 643-0884
Email: admissions@berkeley.edu

COST OF ATTENDANCE:

In-State Tuition & Fees: $14,254 | **Additional Expenses:** $25,296
Total: $39,550

Out-of-State Tuition & Fees: $44,008 | **Additional Expenses:** $25,296
Total: $69,304

Financial Aid: https://admissions.berkeley.edu/types-of-aid

ADDITIONAL INFORMATION:

Available Degree(s)

- B.A. Architecture

Graduate Degree(s)

- Master of Architecture (M.Arch.)
- Master of Advanced Architectural Design (M.A.A.D)
- M.S. Architecture
- Ph.D. Architecture

Portfolio Requirement

There is no portfolio requirement for incoming first-year students.

Scholarships Offered

The Berkeley Undergraduate Scholarship recognizes CA residents based on academic merit. In addition, the Regents' and Chancellor's Scholarship offers at least $2,500 per year.

Special Opportunities

There are two tracks for BA Architecture students to choose from: Design Research or Studio. The Design Research track has fourth-year students exploring two different themes throughout the year. The studio track is studio-intensive and requires that students choose between an energy & the environment or construction course in their last year.

Notable Alumni

Yahya Abdul-Mateen II, Austin Allen, Diane Jones Allen, Mai K. Arbegast, Shlomo Aronson, William Byrd Callaway, Topher Delaney, Orlando Diaz-Azcuy, Garrett Eckbo, Asa Hanamoto, Mark Owen Francis, Christophe Girot, Richard Haag, Ron Herman, Walter Hood, Daniel Iacofano, Elyse Keaton, Diane Kostial, Clare Cooper Marcus, Michael R. Painter, Moura Quayle, Robert Royston, Mario G. Schjetnan, Achva Benzinberg Stein, Will Vinton, Francis Violich, Peter Walker, Kim Wilkie, and John L. Wong

ALASKA

ARIZONA

CALIFORNIA

COLORADO

HAWAII

IDAHO

MONTANA

NEVADA

NEW MEXICO

OREGON

UTAH

WASHINGTON

WYOMING

WEST

ALASKA

ARIZONA

CALIFORNIA

COLORADO

HAWAII

IDAHO

MONTANA

NEVADA

NEW MEXICO

OREGON

UTAH

WASHINGTON

WYOMING

UNIVERSITY OF CALIFORNIA, LOS ANGELES

Address: 405 Hilgard Avenue, Los Angeles, CA 90095
Website: *https://www.aud.ucla.edu/academics/undergraduate*
Contact: *https://admission.ucla.edu/contact*
Phone: (310) 206-8441
Email: https://admission.ucla.edu/contact/admission-representatives

COST OF ATTENDANCE:

In-State Tuition & Fees: $13,239 | **Additional Expenses:** $22,096
Total: $35,335

Out-of-State Tuition & Fees: $42,993 | **Additional Expenses:** $22,096
Total: $65,089

Financial Aid: https://www.financialaid.ucla.edu/

ADDITIONAL INFORMATION:

Available Degree(s)

- B.A. Architectural Studies - 2-year

Graduate Degree(s)

- Master of Architecture (M.Arch.)
- M.S. Architecture and Urban Design
- M.A./Ph.D. Architecture

Portfolio Requirement

There is no portfolio requirement for incoming first-year students.

Scholarships Offered

Students may apply for scholarships through the MyUCLA portal. Additionally, UCLA offers the Regents Scholarship for students who demonstrate academic excellence. Up to 100 are awarded per year.

Special Opportunities

Although a 2-year program, students may only enter the major in their junior year at UCLA. Coursework is in critical studies, technology and design. UCLA hosts summer programs such as JumpStart and TeenArch Studio for high school students interested in the architecture field.

Notable Alumni

Rebecca L. Binder, Pamela Grace Burton, Frederick Fisher, Stephen Francis Jones, Alan Hess, Elena Manferdini, Gwynne Pugh, Jay Marshall Strabala, Patrick Tighe, Tom Wiscombe, and Pinar Yoldas

UNIVERSITY OF SOUTHERN CALIFORNIA (USC)

Address: Watt Hall, Suite 204, Los Angeles, CA 90089
Website: *https://arch.usc.edu/*
Contact: *http://departmentsdirectory.usc.edu/*
Phone: (213) 740-2723
Email: archcomm@usc.edu

COST OF ATTENDANCE:

Tuition & Fees: $60,275 | **Additional Expenses:** $18,788
Total: $79,063

Financial Aid: https://financialaid.usc.edu/undergraduates/students.html

ADDITIONAL INFORMATION:

Available Degree(s)

- B.A. Architecture
- Bachelor of Architecture (B.Arch.) - 5-year

Graduate Degree(s)

- Master of Advanced Architectural Studies (M.A.A.S.)
- Master of Building Science (M.B.S.)

Portfolio Requirement

Portfolios are required. Submit 6-12 of your strongest works via SlideRoom.

Scholarships Offered

USC offers several scholarships for all students. The Mork Family Scholarship offers a full tuition award plus a $5,000 stipend. The Trustee Scholarship offers full tuition. In addition, the Presidential Scholarship includes a half tuition award.

Special Opportunities

Students may participate in various study abroad opportunities. Locations and programs vary by year, however previous destinations included cities in Europe, Asia, Latin America, and domestic travel.

Notable Alumni

Gregory Ain, Barry Berkus, Conrad Buff III, Boris Dramov, Behnaz Farahi, Frank O. Gehry, Donald C. Hensman, Alvin Huang, Jon Jerde, Edward Killingsworth, Pierre Koenig, William Krisel, Mark Lee, Thom Mayne, Albert Nozaki, Raphael Soriano, Calvin C. Straub, Paul Revere Williams, and Zelma Wilson

ALASKA

ARIZONA

CALIFORNIA

COLORADO

HAWAII

IDAHO

MONTANA

NEVADA

NEW MEXICO

OREGON

UTAH

WASHINGTON

WYOMING

WEST

ALASKA

ARIZONA

CALIFORNIA

COLORADO

HAWAII

IDAHO

MONTANA

NEVADA

NEW MEXICO

OREGON

UTAH

WASHINGTON

WYOMING

UNIVERSITY OF OREGON

Address: 5249 University of Oregon, Eugene, OR 97403
Website: *https://archenvironment.uoregon.edu/*
Contact: *https://archenvironment.uoregon.edu/about/leadership*
Phone: (541) 346-3656
Email: archinfo@uoregon.edu

COST OF ATTENDANCE:

In-State Tuition & Fees: $15,054 | **Additional Expenses:** $14,640
Total: $29,694

Out-of-State Tuition & Fees: $41,700 | **Additional Expenses:** $14,640
Total: $56,340

Financial Aid: https://financialaid.uoregon.edu/

ADDITIONAL INFORMATION:

Available Degree(s)

- Bachelor of Architecture (B.Arch.) - 5-year
- Bachelor of Landscape Architecture (B.L.A.)
- Bachelor of Interior Architecture

Graduate Degree(s)

- Master of Architecture (M.Arch.)
- M.S. Architecture
- Ph.D. Architecture

Portfolio Requirement

Portfolios are optional for first year applicants. However, they are strongly encouraged. Portfolios should demonstrate creativity and may include a variety of media, such as photography, drawing, sketching, painting, woodworking, architectural-based projects, etc.

Scholarships Offered

The Architects Foundation Diversity Scholarships, need-based aid, and university-wide scholarships offer varying award amounts and opportunities. University-wide scholarships include the Stamps Scholarship (four years of full tuition, fees, room & board, and up to $12,000 in enrichment funds), the Presidential Scholarship ($36,000 over four years), Diversity Excellence Scholarship ($6500), and more.

Special Opportunities

B.Arch. students must begin coursework in the Eugene, OR campus first. Once the prerequisites have been completed, they may continue their degree work at the Portland, OR campus. University of Oregon houses numerous facilities for architecture students to utilize, such as the woodshop, the studio shop, the Baker Lighting Lab, fabrication labs, and more.

Notable Alumni

Muzharul Islam, Rick Mather, and Eugene Tssui

UNIVERSITY OF WASHINGTON

Address: University of Washington, Seattle, WA 98195
Website: *https://arch.be.uw.edu/programs-and-courses/ba-arch-2/*
Contact: *https://admit.washington.edu/contact/*
Phone: (206) 543-9686
Email: Contact via contact link.

COST OF ATTENDANCE:

In-State Tuition & Fees: $12,076 | **Additional Expenses:** $18,564
Total: $30,640

Out-of-State Tuition & Fees: $39,906 | **Additional Expenses:** $18,564
Total: $58,470

Financial Aid: https://www.washington.edu/financialaid/

ADDITIONAL INFORMATION:

Available Degree(s)

- B.A. Architecture
- B.A. Architectural Design

Portfolio Requirement

Portfolios are required. Include 12-24 pages of design work.

Scholarships Offered

UW offers several types of institutional aid for all students. Washington residents that show exceptional leadership and community engagement may be eligible for the Presidential Scholarship (valued at $10,000). All U.S. citizens may be eligible for the Purple & Gold Scholarship. High-need, high achieving students are eligible for the UW Diversity Scholarship ($10,000 per year for four years).

Special Opportunities

UW offers a dual degree program where students may earn a B.A. in Architectural Design and a B.S. in Construction Management in five years.

Notable Alumni

Wang Chiu-Hwa, Steven Holl, Patricia J. Lancaster, George Nakashima, Victor Steinbrueck, and Minoru Yamasaki

ALASKA

ARIZONA

CALIFORNIA

COLORADO

HAWAII

IDAHO

MONTANA

NEVADA

NEW MEXICO

OREGON

UTAH

WASHINGTON

WYOMING

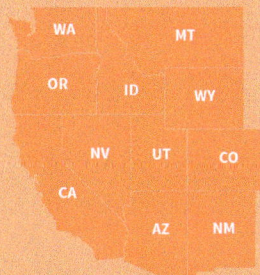

WEST

CHAPTER 15

ARCHITECTURE SCHOOLS ALPHABETIZED BY CITY/STATE

Architecture School	City	State
Auburn University	Auburn	Alabama
Tuskegee University	Tuskegee	Alabama
University of Arizona	Tuscon	Arizona
University of Arkansas	Fayetteville	Arkansas
University of California, Berkeley	Berkeley	California
Southern California Institute of Architecture (SCI-Arc)	Los Angeles	California
University of California, Los Angeles (UCLA)	Los Angeles	California
University of Southern California (USC)	Los Angeles	California
California State Polytechnic University, Pomona (Cal Poly Pomona)	Pomona	California
California College of the Arts (CCA)	San Francisco	California
California Polytechnic State University, San Luis Obispo (Cal Poly SLO)	San Luis Obispo	California
Yale University	New Haven	Connecticut
Howard University	Washington	D.C.
University of Miami	Coral Gables	Florida
Florida Atlantic University	Ft. Lauderdale	Florida
University of Florida, Gainesville	Gainesville	Florida
Florida A&M University	Tallahassee	Florida
Georgia Institute of Technology	Atlanta	Georgia
Savannah College of Art and Design (SCAD)	Savannah	Georgia
University of Illinois Urbana-Champaign (UIUC)	Champaign	Illinois
Illinois Institute of Technology	Chicago	Illinois
University of Notre Dame	Notre Dame	Indiana
Iowa State University	Ames	Iowa
Louisiana State University (LSU)	Baton Rouge	Louisiana
Tulane University	New Orleans	Louisiana
Boston Architectural College	Boston	Massachusetts
Northeastern University	Boston	Massachusetts
Harvard University	Cambridge	Massachusetts
Massachusetts Institute of Technology (MIT)	Cambridge	Massachusetts
University of Michigan	Ann Arbor	Michigan
University of Minnesota	Minneapolis	Minnesota
Washington University in St. Louis	St. Louis	Missouri
New Jersey Institute of Technology (NJIT)	Newark	New Jersey
Princeton University	Princeton	New Jersey
SUNY College of Technology at Alfred State University	Alfred	New York
Pratt Institute	Brooklyn	New York

Architecture School	City	State
Cornell University	Ithaca	New York
The City College of New York - CUNY	New York	New York
The Cooper Union	New York	New York
New York Institute of Technology (NYIT)	Old Westbury	New York
Syracuse University	Syracuse	New York
Rensselaer Polytechnic Institute (RPI)	Troy	New York
University of North Carolina at Charlotte	Charlotte	North Carolina
North Carolina State University (NC State)	Raleigh	North Carolina
University of Oklahoma	Norman	Oklahoma
Oklahoma State University	Stillwater	Oklahoma
University of Oregon	Eugene	Oregon
Thomas Jefferson University	Philadelphia	Pennsylvania
University of Pennsylvania (UPenn)	Philadelphia	Pennsylvania
Carnegie Mellon University	Pittsburgh	Pennsylvania
Pennsylvania State University (Penn State)	University Park	Pennsylvania
Rhode Island School of Design (RISD)	Providence	Rhode Island
The University of Tennessee, Knoxville	Knoxville	Tennessee
The University of Texas at Austin (UT Austin)	Austin	Texas
Texas A&M University	College Station	Texas
Rice University	Houston	Texas
University of Houston	Houston	Texas
Virginia Polytechnic State University	Blacksburg	Virginia
University of Virginia	Charlottesville	Virginia
University of Washington	Seattle	Washington

CHAPTER 16

TOP 20 ARCHITECTURE SCHOOLS

Ranking	School
1	Cornell University
2	Rhode Island School of Design
3	Rice University
4	Cooper Union for the Advancement of Science and Art
5	Syracuse University
6	Carnegie Mellon University
7	Cal Poly San Luis Obispo
8	University of Texas at Austin
9	Massachusetts Institute of Technology
10	Georgia Institute of Technology
11	Pratt Institute
12	Illinois Institute of Technology
13	Northeastern University
14	Washington University in St. Louis
15	University of Southern California
16	Southern California Institute of Architecture
17	Auburn University
18	Rensselaer Polytechnic Institute
19	Virginia Tech
20	Pennsylvania State University

CHAPTER 17

ARCHITECTURE SCHOOLS BY AVERAGE GPA

School	Avg. GPA
Tuskegee University	3
The City College of New York - CUNY	3.34
New York Institute of Technology (NYIT)	3.4
University of Arizona	3.43
Louisiana State University (LSU)	3.45
Florida A&M University	3.5
Howard University	3.55
New Jersey Institute of Technology (NJIT)	3.59
Oklahoma State University	3.59
Savannah College of Art and Design (SCAD)	3.6
University of Miami	3.6
University of Oklahoma	3.63
Tulane University	3.64
University of Oregon	3.65
Syracuse University	3.67
Iowa State University	3.71
University of Houston	3.73
Florida Atlantic University	3.74
The Cooper Union	3.75
University of Arkansas	3.75
North Carolina State University (NC State)	3.8
Pratt Institute	3.82
University of Washington	3.82
University of Southern California (USC)	3.83
Carnegie Mellon University	3.85
University of California, Berkeley	3.87
University of Michigan	3.87
University of Florida, Gainesville	3.88
University of California, Los Angeles (UCLA)	3.9
University of Pennsylvania (UPenn)	3.9
Rensselaer Polytechnic Institute (RPI)	3.91
University of North Carolina at Charlotte	3.92
Princeton University	3.93
The University of Tennessee, Knoxville	3.96
Virginia Polytechnic State University	3.96
Auburn University	3.97
California Polytechnic State University, San Luis Obispo (Cal Poly SLO)	3.99

School	Avg. GPA
Georgia Institute of Technology	4.09
Washington University in St. Louis	4.21
Harvard University	4.22
University of Virginia	4.31
California College of the Arts (CCA)	N/A
California State Polytechnic University, Pomona (Cal Poly Pomona)	N/A
Cornell University	N/A
Illinois Institute of Technology	N/A
Massachusetts Institute of Technology (MIT)	N/A
Northeastern University	N/A
Pennsylvania State University (Penn State)	N/A
Rhode Island School of Design (RISD)	N/A
Rice University	N/A
Southern California Institute of Architecture (SCI-Arc)	N/A
SUNY College of Technology at Alfred State University	N/A
Texas A&M University	N/A
The University of Texas at Austin (UT Austin)	N/A
Thomas Jefferson University	N/A
University of Illinois Urbana-Champaign (UIUC)	N/A
University of Minnesota	N/A
University of Notre Dame	N/A
Yale University	N/A
Boston Architectural College	N/A *Open admissions

ARCHITECTURE SCHOOLS BY AVERAGE SAT SCORE

School	Avg. SAT
Tuskegee University	450-525 (ERW) 410-520 (M)
SUNY College of Technology at Alfred State University	470-580 (ERW) 470-590 (M)
Iowa State University	480-630 (ERW) 530-680 (M)
Southern California Institute of Architecture (SCI-Arc)	499-651 (ERW) 500-685 (M)
California State Polytechnic University, Pomona (Cal Poly Pomona)	500-610 (ERW) 510-640 (M)
Florida A&M University	520-590 (ERW) 510-560 (M)
The City College of New York - CUNY	520-610 (ERW) 530-650 (M)
New York Institute of Technology (NYIT)	520-630 (ERW) 540-660 (M)
Florida Atlantic University	540-620 (ERW) 520-600 (M)
Savannah College of Art and Design (SCAD)	540-640 (ERW) 500-600 (M)
Oklahoma State University	540-640 (ERW) 520-640 (M)
Thomas Jefferson University	550-630 (ERW) 540-640 (M)
University of Arkansas	550-640 (ERW) 540-640 (M)
University of Oregon	550-650 (ERW) 540-640 (M)
Louisiana State University (LSU)	550-660 (ERW) 540-640 (M)
University of Arizona	550-660 (ERW) 540-690 (M)
University of North Carolina at Charlotte	560-640 (ERW) 560-640 (M)
University of Oklahoma	560-650 (ERW) 540-650 (M)
University of Houston	560-650 (ERW) 560-660 (M)
Pratt Institute	570-660 (ERW) 550-680 (M)
Illinois Institute of Technology	570-670 (ERW) 620-730 (M)
Howard University	580-640 (ERW) 550-620 (M)
The University of Tennessee, Knoxville	580-650 (ERW) 560-653 (M)
Pennsylvania State University (Penn State)	580-670 (ERW) 580-700 (M)
Texas A&M University	580-680 (ERW) 580-800 (M)
Auburn University	590-650 (ERW) 580-680 (M)
New Jersey Institute of Technology (NJIT)	590-670 (ERW) 610-720 (M)
Virginia Polytechnic State University	590-680 (ERW) 580-690 (M)
University of Washington	590-700 (ERW) 610-753 (M)
University of Illinois Urbana-Champaign (UIUC)	590-700 (ERW) 620-770 (M)
University of Minnesota	600-700 (ERW) 640-760 (M)
California Polytechnic State University, San Luis Obispo (Cal Poly SLO)	610-690 (ERW) 610-720 (M)
Rhode Island School of Design (RISD)	610-700 (ERW) 640-770 (M)
The University of Texas at Austin (UT Austin)	610-720 (ERW) 600-750 (M)
North Carolina State University (NC State)	620-690 (ERW) 630-730 (M)

School	Avg. SAT
University of Miami	620-700 (ERW) 630-720 (M)
Rensselaer Polytechnic Institute (RPI)	620-720 (ERW) 680-780 (M)
University of Florida, Gainesville	650-720 (ERW) 640-740 (M)
University of California, Los Angeles (UCLA)	650-740 (ERW) 640-780 (M)
University of California, Berkeley	650-740 (ERW) 660-790 (M)
The Cooper Union	650-740 (ERW) 655-790 (M)
University of Virginia	660-740 (ERW) 660-770 (M)
University of Michigan	660-740 (ERW) 680-780 (M)
University of Southern California (USC)	660-740 (ERW) 680-790 (M)
Georgia Institute of Technology	670-740 (ERW) 700-790 (M)
Tulane University	680-740 (ERW) 680-770 (M)
Cornell University	680-750 (ERW) 720-790 (M)
Northeastern University	690-750 (ERW) 720-790 (M)
University of Notre Dame	690-760 (ERW) 710-790 (M)
Carnegie Mellon University	700-760 (ERW) 760-800 (M)
Princeton University	710-770 (ERW) 740-800 (M)
Rice University	710-770 (ERW) 750-800 (M)
University of Pennsylvania (UPenn)	710-770 (ERW) 750-800 (M)
Washington University in St. Louis	720-760 (ERW) 760-800 (M)
Harvard University	720-780 (ERW) 740-800 (M)
Yale University	720-780 (ERW) 740-800 (M)
Massachusetts Institute of Technology (MIT)	730-780 (ERW) 780-800 (M)
Syracuse University	N/A
Boston Architectural College	N/A *Open admissions
California College of the Arts (CCA)	N/A *Test optional

ARCHITECTURE SCHOOLS BY AVERAGE ACT SCORE

School	Avg. ACT
Tuskegee University	18-24
SUNY College of Technology at Alfred State University	18-25
California State Polytechnic University, Pomona (Cal Poly Pomona)	19-27
Florida A&M University	20-24
Savannah College of Art and Design (SCAD)	20-27
Thomas Jefferson University	20-27
Florida Atlantic University	21-26
Iowa State University	21-28
University of Arizona	21-29
Howard University	22-26
University of North Carolina at Charlotte	22-27
Oklahoma State University	22-28
University of Houston	22-28
University of Oregon	22-29
Louisiana State University (LSU)	23-28
University of Arkansas	23-29
University of Oklahoma	23-29
New York Institute of Technology (NYIT)	23-30
The City College of New York - CUNY	23-31
Auburn University	24-30
Pennsylvania State University (Penn State)	25-30
Pratt Institute	25-30
New Jersey Institute of Technology (NJIT)	25-31
The University of Tennessee, Knoxville	25-31
University of Minnesota	25-31
Virginia Polytechnic State University	25-31
California Polytechnic State University, San Luis Obispo (Cal Poly SLO)	26-32
Illinois Institute of Technology	26-32
Texas A&M University	26-32
The University of Texas at Austin (UT Austin)	26-33
Southern California Institute of Architecture (SCI-Arc)	27-30
North Carolina State University (NC State)	27-32
Rhode Island School of Design (RISD)	27-32
University of Illinois Urbana-Champaign (UIUC)	27-33
University of Washington	27-33
University of Miami	28-32

School	Avg. ACT
University of Florida, Gainesville	29-33
Rensselaer Polytechnic Institute (RPI)	29-34
University of California, Los Angeles (UCLA)	29-34
Tulane University	30-33
University of Southern California (USC)	30-34
University of Virginia	30-34
The Cooper Union	30-35
University of California, Berkeley	30-35
University of Michigan	31-34
Georgia Institute of Technology	31-35
Cornell University	32-35
Princeton University	32-35
University of Notre Dame	32-35
Harvard University	33-35
Yale University	33-35
Carnegie Mellon University	33-35
University of Pennsylvania (UPenn)	33-35
Washington University in St. Louis	33-35
Rice University	34-36
Massachusetts Institute of Technology (MIT)	34-36
Northeastern University	34-36
Syracuse University	N/A
Boston Architectural College	N/A *Open admissions
California College of the Arts (CCA)	N/A *Test optional

JOURNEY TO ARCHITECTURE, ART, DANCE, MUSIC, THEATRE, FILM, AND FASHION SERIES

JOURNEY TO
Fashion Design
COLLEGE ADMISSIONS & PROFILES

RACHEL A. WINSTON, PH.D.

JOURNEY TO
Fashion Merchandising
COLLEGE ADMISSIONS & PROFILES

RACHEL A. WINSTON, PH.D.

JOURNEY TO
Costume Design & Technical Theatre
COLLEGE ADMISSIONS & PROFILES

RACHEL A. WINSTON, PH.D.

JOURNEY TO
Theatre and the Dramatic Arts
COLLEGE ADMISSIONS & PROFILES

RACHEL A. WINSTON, PH.D.

JOURNEY TO
Musical
Theatre
COLLEGE ADMISSIONS & PROFILES

STAGE DOOR

RACHEL A. WINSTON, PH.D.

Live your dreams today remembering that discipline is the bridge between dreams and achievement!

"We believe in the American Dream that all people rich or poor can go as far in life as their talents and persistence will take them."

– Lizard Publishing Vision

At Lizard, we help you make your dreams come true.

CONTACT INFORMATION

Phone: 949-833-7706

E-mail: collegeguide@yahoo.com

Website: collegelizard.com and Lizard-publishing.com

COMPREHENSIVE HEALTH CARE SERIES

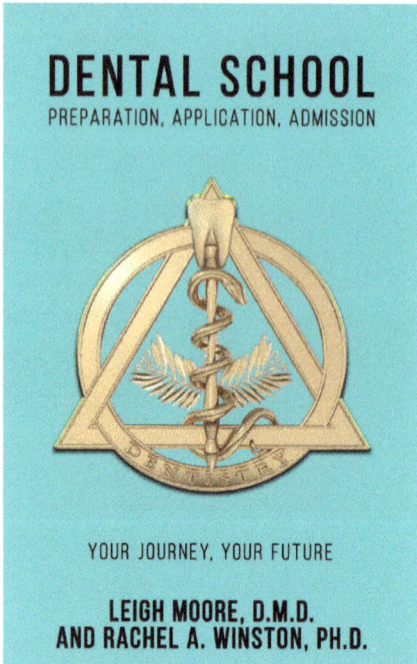

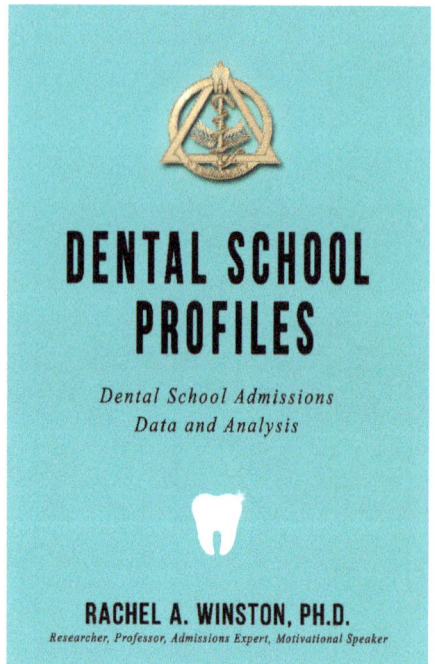

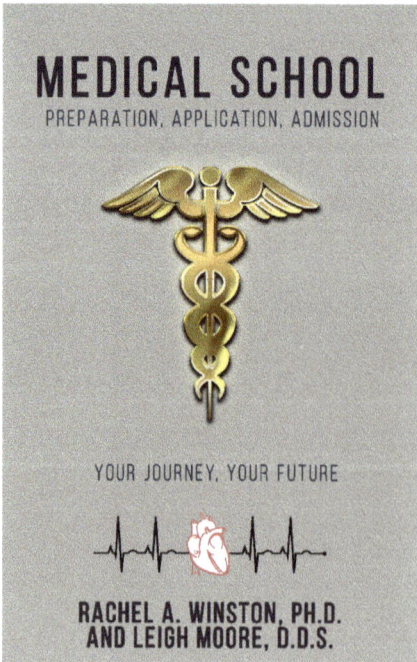

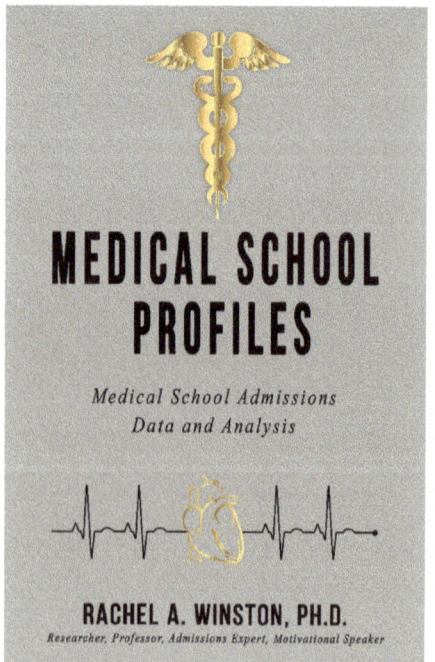

DENTAL SCHOOL
PREPARATION, APPLICATION, ADMISSION

YOUR JOURNEY, YOUR FUTURE

**LEIGH MOORE, D.M.D.
AND RACHEL A. WINSTON, PH.D.**

DENTAL SCHOOL PROFILES

*Dental School Admissions
Data and Analysis*

RACHEL A. WINSTON, PH.D.
Researcher, Professor, Admissions Expert, Motivational Speaker

MEDICAL SCHOOL
PREPARATION, APPLICATION, ADMISSION

YOUR JOURNEY, YOUR FUTURE

**RACHEL A. WINSTON, PH.D.
AND LEIGH MOORE, D.D.S.**

MEDICAL SCHOOL PROFILES

*Medical School Admissions
Data and Analysis*

RACHEL A. WINSTON, PH.D.
Researcher, Professor, Admissions Expert, Motivational Speaker

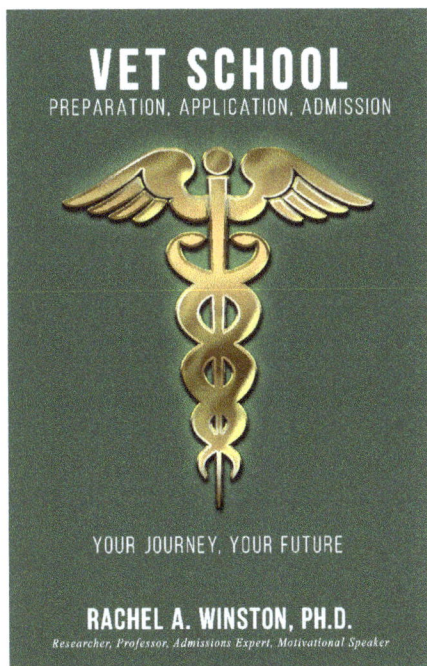

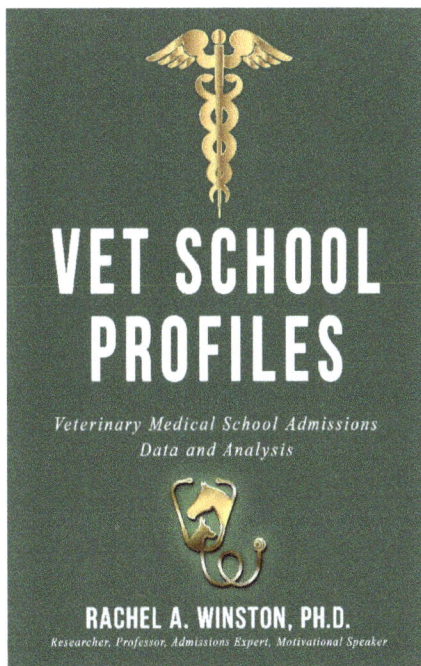

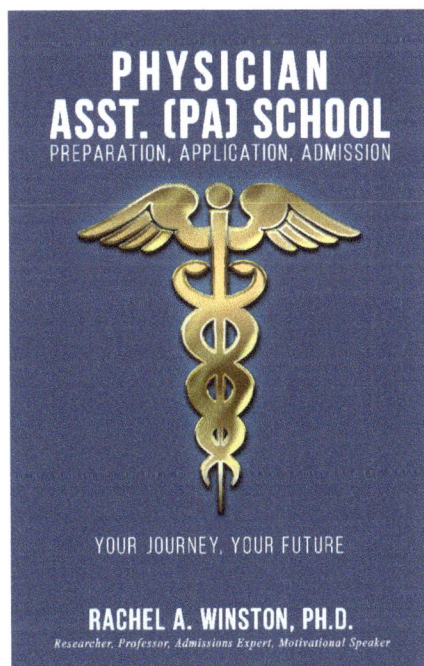

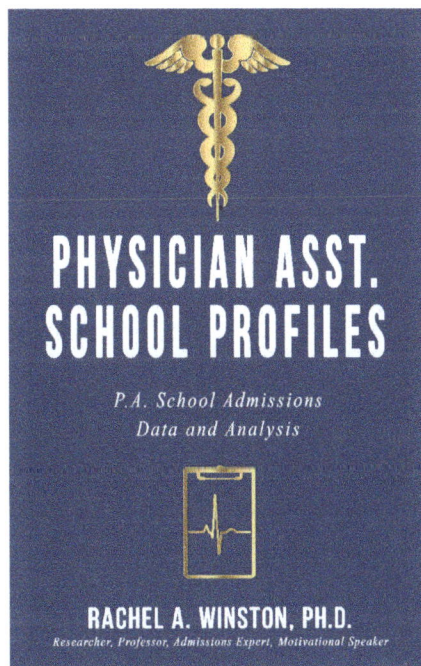

PHARM.D. SCHOOL
PREPARATION, APPLICATION, ADMISSION

YOUR JOURNEY, YOUR FUTURE

RACHEL A. WINSTON, PH.D.
Researcher, Professor, Admissions Expert, Motivational Speaker

PHARM.D. SCHOOL PROFILES

Pharmacy School Admissions Data and Analysis

RACHEL A. WINSTON, PH.D.
Researcher, Professor, Admissions Expert, Motivational Speaker

OSTEOPATHIC MEDICAL SCHOOL
PREPARATION, APPLICATION, ADMISSION

YOUR JOURNEY, YOUR FUTURE

RACHEL A. WINSTON, PH.D.
Researcher, Professor, Admissions Expert, Motivational Speaker

OSTEO SCHOOL PROFILES

Osteopathic Medical School Admissions Data and Analysis

RACHEL A. WINSTON, PH.D.
Researcher, Professor, Admissions Expert, Motivational Speaker

INDEX

A

C

G

H

I

M

N

P

R

www.ingramcontent.com/pod-product-compliance
Lightning Source LLC
Chambersburg PA
CBHW052017030426

42335CB00026B/3174